CANADA'S FLOWERS

HISTORY OF THE CORVETTES OF CANADA

BY THOMAS G. LYNCH

Merry Christmas
Dad
1988
Love Jay

Published by Nimbus Publishing Limited, P.O. Box 9301, Station A Halifax, Nova Scotia, B3K 5N5 (1982)
ISBN 0-920852-15-7
First edition published by International Graphics Corp., Bennington VT 05201 (1980)
Fourth Printing, 1983
Fifth Printing, 1987

TABLE OF CONTENTS

PREFACE

In researching this 'Special' on the corvettes of Canada's Navy during the years of the Second World War, I was struck by the amount that had been written about them, but how little was really said that was of use to the average modeler or serious military researcher/historian. What was written was largely about British corvettes, with passing reference to Canadian warships of the same class. I did not consider this to be right.

The corvette was the largest escort class ever built, bar none, and by war's end had changed the Royal Canadian Navy (RCN) of the time into a first-class naval force. They took an infantile shipbuilding industry and brought it to the point where major ships could be built, both during and after the war. They, with their inherent shortcomings, came to typify the young RCN, with their largely volunteer crews and officers, who by war's end had become the most important components in the struggle that was to be called the "Battle of the Atlantic." Other ships, such as the new Tribals (destroyers) were to make inroads with the Canadian public, through the press and radio networks, but the chubby corvette was the vessel that saved the day through those black years of the 1940-44 period, when all seemed to go wrong for the Allies.

To the men and officers of these sturdy, little ships I would like to dedicate this work. I hope it goes a little way to show the spirit and conditions they lived under and the battles they fought against the U-boat, the tedium, and the ever-present enemy, the North Atlantic.

Thomas G. Lynch
Guysborough, Nova Scotia, Canada
September 1980

INTRODUCTION

This book is, quite literally, a unique story about a unique ship.

The corvette, of course, was itself unique, born of a particular necessity at a particular moment; nothing like her had ever been seen before, nothing quite like her will ever be seen again.

But the book is unique in that it sets forth, in great detail, the peculiar role that this class of ship played in the development of a nation, the contribution of the corvette to the winning of the Battle of the Atlantic has been chronicled before, but here in this book the author examines, for the first time, the distinctively Canadian aspects of the corvette fleets of World War Two.

For the British and Allied navies, the corvette, however useful, was a stop-gap, a "hostilities only" expedient used to fill out the escort forces worn desperately thin by the wartime attrition of the traditional destroyer flotillas. But for Canada, the corvette assumed an infinitely greater significance. It was the first warship the country had ever built in any numbers; with the corvette, Canadian shipbuilding established itself, so that at the war's end a complex of shipyards had been founded, inland as well as on both coasts, and a reservoir of skills and expertise had been established which would become the basis of a vital and significant national industry.

Even more important was the role of this wartime class of ship in the development of Canada's national navy. As the trickle of these fat-funnelled, duck-sterned, jaunty little vessels grew to a flood in the mid-war years when the newly-established shipyards settled into their stride, the Royal Canadian Navy grew from a clutch of venerable destroyers manned by a handful of peacetime professionals, to an enormous force of nearly a hundred thousand men and women, manning a fleet of hundreds of ships which was the third largest Allied navy and a decisive element in the global balance of power.

But far and away the most important Canadian contribution of the wartime corvette was to the nation's coming of age. In the messdecks and wardrooms of the wartime escort groups a new generation of Canadians came face to face with the harsh realities of their world, stripped bare of the comforting illusions of peacetime living. Here were shaped the character and outlook of the men who would one day play a key role in the running of a vigorous, developing nation, while their government ashore grappled, for the first time, with the responsibilities of exercising power on a global, and not merely a domestic, scale. With its new-built navy Canada had entered the corridors of power, and for all Canadians it was a heady experience that would never be forgotten. It is no exaggeration to say that the corvette played a significant role, not only in the winning of the greatest, longest and costliest battle ever fought, but in the shaping of the Canadian nation.

It is this Canadian aspect of this remarkable little warship which is chronicled in these pages, and which makes them a unique contribution to the naval history of the world.

James B. Lamb

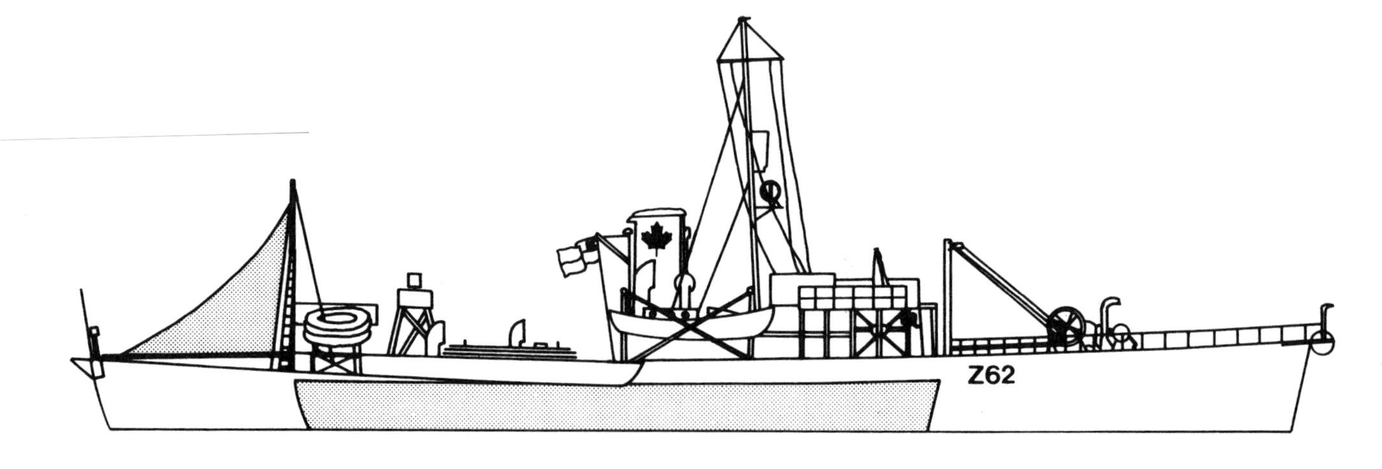

HMCS SACKVILLE June 1945

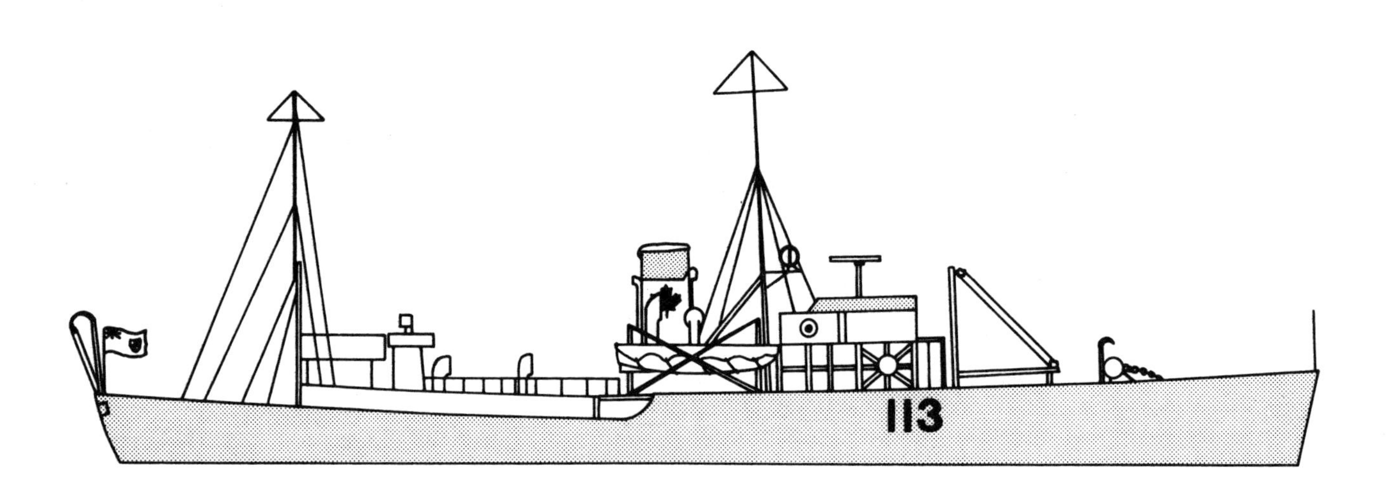

HMCS SACKVILLE February 1961

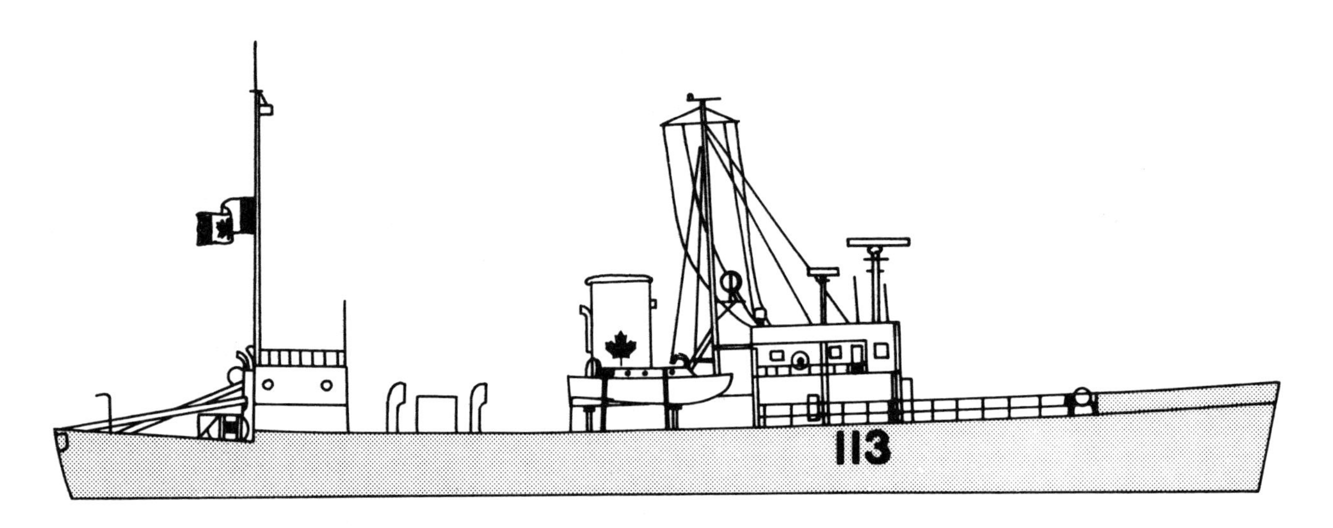

CFAV SACKVILLE 1980

Although out of context, this photo shows Alan Easton's BADDECK to good advantage. The 271 radar is evident in front of mast, as well as the Canadian Maple Leaf, which appeared on Canadian units as early as 1943, to distinguish these from Royal Navy units. Note the extended forecastle. The camouflage is 1943 Western Approaches scheme (light green, light blue, and light gray or off-white). Note the star rocket rails on the 4-inch gun shield. [Author's collection]

CONCEPTION

The idea or concept of the corvette was born of the Munich Crisis of 1938, which convinced enough members of the British Admiralty Board that war with the Third Reich was inevitable. Plans were drawn up that would put Britain and her armed forces on a war footing by 1940, but the problem of close escort vessels to be used within coastal waters had to be solved in some way. Existing warships and their design were far too complex and the major shipbuilders' yards were filled to capacity with other ship orders as well.

Mr. William Reed, of Smith's Dock Company at Southbank on the Tees had vast experience with whaling vessels for all waters. When Admiralty specifications for small coastal escorts were called, he advanced a proposal based on a recent whaling ship built by Smith's; the *Southern Pride*. He combined his experience building small patrol vessels during the "Great War" with the *Southern Pride*'s specifications, and submitted these to the Admiralty, calling it "Patrol Vessel, Whaler Type". It was to be 205 feet overall, a beam of 33 feet, and draw 15 feet of water. She would be highly maneuverable, with a single 3-blade propeller, driven by a four-cylinder, triple-expansion reciprocating engine of 2,750 horsepower, in turn fed by two cylindrical Scotch boilers. Everything was to be kept as simple as possible, so that small yards would be able to construct them without major expansion. The vessel would have a range of 4,000 miles on 200 tons of fuel at twelve knots and a maximum speed of 16 knots, which was deemed sufficient for her proposed duties. Her major weapons would be the 300 pound depth charge, dropped over the stern through rails and fired by depth charge throwers. Surface engagement weapons would be limited to a single 4-inch forward and a 2-pounder aft, with Lewis guns to supplement. They were to cost an estimated 90,000 Pounds each, and were later dubbed by Winston Churchill as "cheap, but Nasties".

Admiralty officials and Smith Dockyard designers met in January 1939, and after discarding several other designs, the modified *Southern Pride* design was settled on as the most promising. Contracts and approval were awarded on 27 February, which shows the increasing uneasyness of Admiralty House, as the world situation deteriorated in the last months of peace. Other outstanding specs for the vessel were laid out: 700 tons, and seven months building time. But by October 1939, the plans had grown; an increase to 1,390 tons had been rejected, mainly because it called for coal-fired boilers! For better or worse, the design was finalized at 940 tons (standard), 190 feet between perpendiculars, 33 feet beam, 7 feet 9 inches mean draught (forward), 205 feet overall length, 47 officers and men. This was to be the design that would be mass-produced in various forms for the next four years.

Meanwhile in Canada, 1939 saw her desperately searching for some contribution that she could make to the nearing maritime war. Destroyers had been thought of, but no one shipyard in Canada had ever built anything larger than small minesweepers. The idea was discarded.

However, just days after the outbreak of hostilities in Europe, a set of plans were found of this "Patrol Vessel, Whaler Type" that had been sent by the Admiralty. Within seventy-two hours a proposal was made to Admiralty House that maybe Canadian shipyards were capable of building this type of warship. Really, this was quite a gamble, as Canadian yards had never built anything over a hundred feet long, and never as com-

HMS BEGONIA, completed 8 March 1941, compared to the Smith Whaler SOUTHERN PRIDE, the vessel design that corvettes evolved from. [via author]

plicated. At this point, the vessels of this type were envisioned as protecting the western terminals of the convoy routes, the coastal approaches and the St. Lawrence River and Gulf. Neither Ottawa nor London had any idea of what would develop by 6 June 1940. But the need for ships of this type were foreseen as replacements for other, more important units in convoy waters. The yards of Britain and the United States might not be enough. Canada would have to contribute too.

Along the chain of argument and compromise, Rear Adm. Percy Nelles, Canadian Chief of Staff, suggested that the name 'corvette' be used for this little vessel, as 'patrol vessel, whaler type' was a bit long and wasn't very catchy. The Canadian corvettes were to add a new chapter to the tradition-laden name, with bravery and valor.

Now that Canada was committed to building these "corvettes", the question arose — where? There wasn't time to assess Canadian shipyards and if there had been it would have discouraged the most avid optimist. Lack of workers, lack of *yards*, lack of essential skills and trades and lack of equipment were glaring facts. Materials

The hull of HMCS COLLINGWOOD after launching, 27 July 1940, Collingwood, Ontario. Note the short forecastle, with wood decking in the deck winch area. Small oval hatches are to bunker tanks, large square one will lead to starboard minesweeping gear room, and other to steerage machine shop space. Large rivets show to good advantage on deckhouse structure, but few can be seen on the hull, as these were flush-fitted. Note the timber baulks which she rested on and the small launch space. [Ken MacPherson]

Hull No. 57 which will become HMCS OAKVILLE in November 1941. Already changes to the British pattern are evident on this hull. Anti-roll keels show to good advantage. Canadian designers moved the bandstand where the "pom-pom" would reside aft, to give greater field of fire; galley has been moved forward as well. Note how most were launched sideways, thus negating the need for elaborate slipways. [Ken MacPherson]

HMCS WINDFLOWER: This was one of the very first corvette photos released for publication. Late 1940, as can be seen by crew in duffle coats. Note "Windy" hasn't a 4-inch or anything in her bandstand, which is in the early position as per Admiralty specifications. She was built for the Royal Navy, but reverted to the Royal Canadian Navy. Galley is aft, which meant cold and soggy meals as they had to be carried forward on the open decks. Overall scheme is light gray. [Ken MacPherson]

were non-existant, as war priorities had gobbled up existing stocks of steel, copper, brass, rubber and other essential components. What was necessary was an industrial revolution in Canada and bloody quick, to quote an official of the day!

Another thought that haunted Ottawa: assuming that these corvettes could be built — no one had *any* idea *how* they would work at sea! If these ships should fail in their role or industry in building them, the damage would be incalculable. Manpower, industrial effort, and worst yet: one year's time would be wasted. It would be a naval disaster with world-wide repercussions, if it failed.

However, the gamble was to be taken. The program called for sixty-four corvettes plus ten Bangor Class minesweepers to be built *and* manned in two years. In the future this would be expanded again and again, as Canadian yards became more proficient. But now, first the shipyards had to be built or expanded, then materials to work with, train the workmen, master the skills necessary to build corvettes was the order of the day. Some bill for the miniscule ship industry of Canada in 1939!

By February 1940 the building program was underway in fine style. The RCN had entered the war with seven overworked destroyers, which had very little experience at war, little shore organization, and a tumultuous ship building industry with grave doubts as to its role or ability. But now the Canadian war machine began to gather steam.

The war in the east had quieted down, with the Royal Navy (RN) giving the U-boats a hard time with the Type 123 Asdic, which was much more advanced than German Naval officials had realized. But this was to prove to be the calm before the storm. All hell broke loose in April 1940, with the invasion of Norway and Denmark.

Alan Easton describes his first view of his new corvette, and although this didn't occur until 1941, it illustrates how these small ships affected their young skippers...

"She was resting on the blocks of a drydock in a St. Lawrence River shipyard [Morton's]. I stood on the wall and looked down on this sturdy vessel which was to take me many miles over the ocean. HMCS *Baddeck* was mine: we were to spend a part of our lives together.

"I could see that the ship had been built after the fashion of a big steam trawler, but with a longer and sharper bow. In her nakedness, her fat belly seemed to bulge over the floor of the dry dock, suggesting an ample capacity for, among other things, a large engine. Her

HMCS AGASSIZ, as she appeared in early 1941, still without anti-aircraft armament. Note galley stove-pipe, hidden partially by the signal flag locker. Bandstand is further aft. AGASSIZ was one of the few completed with the mainmast, which was necessary for the British-type long range radio and its aerials. Note also the Mark II minesweeping gear aft. Radio specified for this ship was the type TW12b, but was never fitted. The first 54 Canadian corvettes were outfitted with the minesweeping gear. [Ken MacPherson]

Photo taken in 1941 of HMCS BATTLEFORD. Note the mainmast and lack of 2-pounder. [Marcom Museum]

rounded stern was inclined to turn up like a duck's tail..."

In Canada the last months of 1940 saw the passage down the St. Lawrence of fourteen small, half-equipped, skeleton-crewed warships.[1] These were the first Canadian corvettes to be finished. They were late being completed, but built they were. These were to proceed to England with all possible haste, and since there was a shortage of 4-inch guns in Canada, wooden 'dummies' were fitted for the North Atlantic crossing. *Windflower* and *Mayflower* were the first to cross in January 1941. Terence Robertson, serving on a destroyer in the mid-Atlantic, writes:

> "She was Canadian-built, Canadian-manned and named *Windflower.* When the destroyer in which I was serving met this newcomer to the Atlantic battlefield in January 1941, we not unnaturally approached for a closer look. We saw on foredeck a wooden 4-inch gun with a wooden barrel that drooped. Then we were warned to keep clear of her stern with the immortal signal, 'If you touch me there, I'll scream.'"

As the two ships neared the English Western Approaches, they encountered units of the British Home Fleet. The Admiral aboard HMS *Rodney* upon studying *Mayflower* through his glasses, noted upon her drooped barrel thus: "My God! Since when are we clubbing the enemy to death?"

These were the forerunners of 122 corvettes that Canada would build and sail. They would never be handsome ships nor comfortable for their crews, because of their low quarterdeck and open well-deck, they were almost continuously under the 'green' water. As well, ventilation was a problem, and hence condensation built up on the interior bulkheads and deckheads, which kept things in a continuous damp or wet condition. This, combined with the lively action of the ships, with attendant breakage of food items and the inevitable seasickness tended to keep the quarters in a stomach-turning mess during heavy weather. Nevertheless, the crews grew to at least tolerate and in some cases to love them, as they were the only home they would know for the duration.

Designed for a crew of 42 officers and men, this rapidly grew as new armament and equipment was added. From 42 it grew to 58 and then to 80, finally reaching numbers of 93 and in extreme examples to 104. All these in that tiny crew's fo'c's'le! (More on this later.)

These were the first. Shipyards in the Maritimes, Quebec, and Ontario, plus the West Coast had improved designs on the drawing boards and the skeletons of numerous new corvettes stood gaunt in Canadian yards. These fourteen, with their icebreaker consort were the untried product. At least Canada could build them!

1. *Arvida, Chambly, Cobalt, Collingwood, Agassiz, Alberni, Arrowhead, Bittersweet, Eyebright, Fennel, Hepatica, Levis, Mayflower, Snowberry.*

DEVELOPMENT

The original, early "Flower" Class corvette derived its name from the suggestion of the Ships' Names Committee that this class of warship follow the old "Herbaceous Border" class of sloop from World War I. It was to prove an unhappy choice for a few corvettes, such as HMS *Pansy, Poppy,* and *Periwinkle*. But in most cases it was a good choice. Canada did not follow suit, other than in a few cases of corvettes transferred from the RN, and named theirs after towns and villages in Canada.

A total of 130 corvettes were built in

Kamsack, part of Western Escort Force, Halifax, June, 1943 [Marcom]

HMCS TRILLIUM, one of the few corvettes which followed the Royal Navy in the practice of naming them after flowers. Note the galley aft and bandstand forward, which appears to have twin .303 machine guns. Note the splinter mats hanging in disarray. [Marcom Museum]

KAMSACK: The bridge has been extended and compass house abolished. The 271P radar is offset to starboard. The lid off the hedgehog on the starboard side, forward of the wing, makes this probably 1944. Three-tone Western Approaches paint scheme shows weathering effects near the waterline, which was common. [Marcom]

Spray thrown over the bridge was common in other than dead-calm conditions. Note the compass house is gone and the gyro compass, binnacle compass, and voice pipes are in the open. The small doors in the forward part of the bridge lead into the chart hut/Asdic room, which forms the bridge front. Note wood planking, the DF loop on bridge front, and rocket illumination rails on the 4-inch. [Canadian Forces photo]

Canada (official figures — 122 actual) but this doesn't mean that an endless stream of standard corvettes flowed down the ways. Continuous changes were made in the design from the time the first corvettes were laid down. Larger and better radios were fitted, radar sets were fitted, including the accursed SW-1 and SW-2 CQ, with their "Fishbone" antenna and the knack of not working when foul or dark, the later 271 P's and 271 Q's, with their distinctive lantern-house housing aft on the bridge, the type 291 air warning radar later again.

The corvette in its original concept was to have operated close to the coast and coastal ocean. However, with developments in 1940, with the fall of France and expansion of the U-boat war, the corvette was pushed into roles it had never been designed for, *but* had the ability to be adapted for. The mast, which had been placed forward to be as far away from the mainmast for the powerful radio aerials, was shifted aft of the wheelhouse after the first 35-40 corvettes. The mainmast, no longer needed, was very easy to omit, after the first fourteen and removed from them at first refit. The compass house was shifted aft, and an open-type bridge position fitted in front. The Asdic hut was shifted to the front and lower position on the bridge. The 271 radar and hut were mounted aft, then the bridge was widened, the radar and hut shifted left or right for better stern coverage (mainly starboard). The compass house was abolished (twice) and the radar moved off the bridge and more toward the ship's center line. Minesweeping gear was standard on the first 54 corvettes (Mk. II) and later removed.

Royal Canadian Navy corvettes remained along RN designs until HMCS *Buctouche*, when the following changes occured: the galley was moved just aft of the C.O.'s cabin, and the separate sleeping and messing quarters were combined. New Canadian-designed radios were installed, being more powerful, and D/F gear was fitted. Bilge keels were fitted to attempt to reduce rolling (it worked).

From Canadian corvette number 61 the forecastle was extended, which gave more crew accomodation and better sea-keeping abilities. All other corvettes eventually had the forecastles extended, but some retained the open well-deck and short forecastle well into 1944.

Armament grew from the basic 4-inch, 2-pounder, to include Lewis guns, replaced by Browning .303 machine guns, replaced by two single 20 mm Oerlikon.

Ships of this caliber now with increased sheer and flare needed a new bridge arrangement. The occasions that had shown corvettes engaged with U-boats at close range with their 4-inch main armament meant that the 4-inch had to be mounted on a raised platform to engage at close range, but this also meant that the bridge had to be raised one deck so the wheelhouse had a clear view over the deck gun. Accordingly the bridge became an open affair atop the wheelhouse platform position, and was later widened to accomodate the 20 mm Oerlikons. The wheelhouse had been raised a deck and this arrangement would be the way things remained for the remaining corvettes.

Improved endurance, better armament, larger displacement, and greater crew size were the upgrading of the corvette. Extended forecastles allowed more room for the crew. Bridge development is shown better in the accompanying line drawings.

An interesting fact is that while the U.S. Navy was reeling from the U-boat onslaught in the spring of 1942, ten corvettes of the RN were transferred to the USN as escort vessels. As well, eight hulls building in Canada were accepted by the Americans. All were classified as gunboats and carried the "PG" designation.

The RN ships became:

Veronica — USS *Temptress* PG62
Heliotrope — USS *Surprise* PG63
Hibiscus — USS *Spry* PG64
Arabis — USS *Saucy* PG65
Periwinkle — USS *Restless* PG66
Calendula — USS *Ready* PG67
Begonia — USS *Impulse* PG68
Larkspur — USS *Fury* PG69
Heartease — USS *Courage* PG70
Candytuft — USS *Tenacity* PG71

The eight Canadian hulls were numbered PG86-96, with hulls returned of seven of fifteen offered. The eight were:

USS *Action* PG86
USS *Alacrity* PG87
USS *Brisk* PG89
USS *Haste* PG92

USS SURPRISE (ex-HMS HELIOTROPE) at Charleston Navy Yard, South Carolina, June 1944. Note the Western Approaches-type paint scheme which looks to be in the standard colors of the U.S. Navy. An American-pattern 4-inch appears forward and 3-inch aft in the bandstand. The open hedgehog is visible forward of the superstructure and appears to be a split version, where there were 12 spigots per unit. [Naval Photographic Center]

Same ship, SURPRISE, showing the aft 3-inch very clearly. The depth charge traps also show very clearly. Note the tripod foremast, retention of a shortened mainmast. [Naval Photographic Center]

USS *Intensity* PG93
USS *Might* PG94
USS *Pert* PG95
USS *Prudent* PG96

American pattern 4 inch and 3 inch anti-aircraft mounts replaced British mounts with some mounting twin 3-inch guns and in general carried more armament than would be tolerated in the RCN. They were used exclusively as coastal escorts and as such served suitably throughout the war. They were returned to the RN at wars' end.

The outstanding features of the Modified Flower Class were the altered hull, a higher bridge, and an upright funnel with a spark screen. The reason for the upright funnel made the inclination of the ship impossible to judge and the screen was necessary to prevent a down-draft of funnel gases. (For further differences, see Appendix I.)

The final outshoot of the 'Flower' Class corvette was, of course, the 'Castle' Class. The outstanding features were increased size, latticed foremast, sharply raked bow, and squared stern. These were all ships built for the RN, but by the time completed the RN had very little need for them. They were loaned to the RCN and all reverted to the RN or were disposed of by 1946.

Eight more of the original fourteen corvettes followed in February 1941, but not for long. The Battle of the Atlantic was spreading westward and these ships were transferred back to the RCN. Spring 1941 also saw success for the RN, with the deaths of Prien, hero of Scapa Flow (at least to the Germans), Schepke rammed and killed in his U-boat by HMS *Vanoc*, and Kretschmer captured and made a POW. *Bismarck* was sunk in May, but during June the U-boats sank 590,000 tons of shipping. Most fore-

USS SAUCY (ex-HMS ARABIS), in May 1942, just after being handed over to the U.S. Navy by the Royal Navy. Note she has the 271 radar, widened bridge, standard BL Mark IX 4-inch and 2-pounder in the original position bandstand. She was one of ten loaned to the U.S. Navy to bolster the Eastern seaboard defenses in the first critical years of America's entry into the war. [Naval Photographic Center]

USS RESTLESS (ex-PERIWINKLE), circa 1945. Note the extreme length of the 4-inch forward mount. These vessels served as coastal escort ships, which was their original intent. They served very well, even though they were considered over-burdened and top-heavy by RCN and RN authorities. All were returned to Britain in 1945. [Naval Photographic Center]

boding was that eleven ships had been sunk within 800 miles of Halifax. The U-boats were in North American waters and there was very little too stop them.

CORVETTES AND THE BATTLE OF THE ATLANTIC

The answer to the problem was that the escort system had to be expanded and westward as well. To do this a huge new naval base would be needed. Halifax was considered, but St. John's, Newfoundland, was 500 miles closer to England and was more favorable in British eyes, with it still being a British protectorate.

The Canadian Navy agreed to operate an escort force from St. John's. Canadian ships in British waters were ordered west to form the Newfoundland Escort Force, under Commodore L. W. Murray. The Command would grow to engulf enormous amounts of ships and men, as well as become the western hinge of the escort-convoy defense.

Meanwhile, the United States had announced its intention to make sure that its shipments got across the Atlantic unmolested. By August 1941 plans included one American ship in each convoy to ensure the assistance of USN ships. By 15 September, the President's "shoot to kill" order directed against U-boats had been issued and cooperation between American warships and ships of the "Newfie" Escort Force were reality.

CORVETTES IN ACTION

The U-boat meanwhile, had acquired an exaggerated respect for the corvettes. A confidential report found after the war reported U-boat commanders "...as boiling with rage at being unable to attack as often as in earlier days owing to increased convoy protection by corvettes...".

U-boats, although faster on the surface and possessed of almost equal firepower, seldom attempted to slug it out with a corvette on the surface, if it could avoid this action.

Thus when a lull occurred in the latter part of the summer 1941, corvette captains took full advantage of this time to train their crews, by making convoy passages to the east with experienced destroyers and their captains.

But the first of September saw the end to the lull. Convoy SC-42 sailed from Sydney, Nova Scotia, on 30 August 1941, carrying over half a million tons of supplies for Britain. The Local Escort handed over to the Newfoundland Escort Force, consisting of HMCS *Skeena* (destroyer escort), the Escort Commander, and the corvettes *Orilla, Kenogami,* and *Alberni.* The course plot called for a course of northeast, up to the latitudes of Cape Farewell (70 degrees north). The convoy contained sixty-four ships and covered twenty-five miles in area.

On the seventh day heavy German radio traffic indicated that German U-boats were in the area and gathering a pack. The convoy swung due north, towards Greenland, which lay dead ahead. But the U-boats were not deceived, and claimed their first victim

CHAMBLY in Halifax harbor, 1941. Note CHAMBLY has the mainmast of the first corvettes. Painted overall medium gray, she has the Mark II minesweeping gear aft. Once again the bandstand is empty, resulting from a shortage of the 2-pounder Vickers "pom-pom". In Canada at this time a shortage of even Lewis guns aggravated the situation. Depth charge thrower shows on quarter-deck, just forward of the bandstand. [Ken MacPherson]

HMCS ALBERNI as she appeared in 1942, type 271 radar fitted to port side of compass platform, bridge extended. Two pounder is trained toward the camera. Note how the galley stack is almost horizontal until the funnel, then up the front side. Note also, how the conning bridge has been extended forward. Lighter area is where censor has removed the "K" number. Also, the compass house has had a "monkey island" added to its top for better look-out. [Author's collection]

at dusk, the freighter *Muneric*. *Kenogami*, on the port side of the convoy reversed course and followed the torpedo tracks in the gathering gloom. Off her starboard bow another torpedo's wake churned through the water, narrowly missing her. The guilty U-boat was finally sighted at 1,000 yards, making for Greenland at high speed. *Kenogami* opened fire, but was recalled, as the Senior Escort had spotted another U-boat dead ahead. Two merchantmen sighted a third U-boat moments later. A fourth was sighted, slipping down between the lines of ships in the convoy, five minutes later. Another merchantman was torpedoed and a third, a tanker, lit up the whole immediate area with flames and debris, much to the U-boat's delight.

At least eight U-boats were involved now, giving the U-boats a two to one advantage over the escort, and the escorts have to pick up survivors as well. Convoy ships were prohibited to stop to assist survivors; the chance of collision or torpedoeing were too great. The destroyer escort and the corvettes did their best with scramble nets and Carley floats, only to be called away to track another U-boat sighting.

A high, white moon turned the seas around into a shooting ground for the U-boats until after midnight. Seven ships were sunk and astern the corvette *Orilla* was endeavoring to assist the tanker *Tahchee*, torpedoed, but still afloat.

A little after 2350 hours, a cloudbank obscured the moon, giving the convoy a chance to alter course. However, before this could be done, machine gun rounds illuminated another U-boat within the convoy. *Skeena* charged into the convoy, chasing the U-boat. However, the U-boat crossed the next column at right angles, reversed course and submerged. *Skeena* was trapped as the convoy executed the delayed turn, and was missed by merchant vessels only by twisting and turning by the desperate captain. As she fought clear, another ship was torpedoed, sending a column of flame 100 feet into the darkened heavens.

Morning brought respite for the exhausted crews, but at about 1200 hours, the *Thistleglen* was torpedoed. But this time *Skeena* had spotted a periscope and raced to place a depth charge pattern on the still-disturbed site. She obtained a poor Asdic contact, but *Alberni* signalled that she had a contact (this was not unusual, as the corvettes were equipped with Type 123 Asdic, and the older destroyer escorts were equipped with older gear). *Kenogami* joined the pair and obtained a contact as well. The three ships began a deliberate attack and after eight depth charge patterns they were rewarded by a large air bubble, followed by large amounts of oil. A probable kill, but still a lick at the U-boats. The rest of the

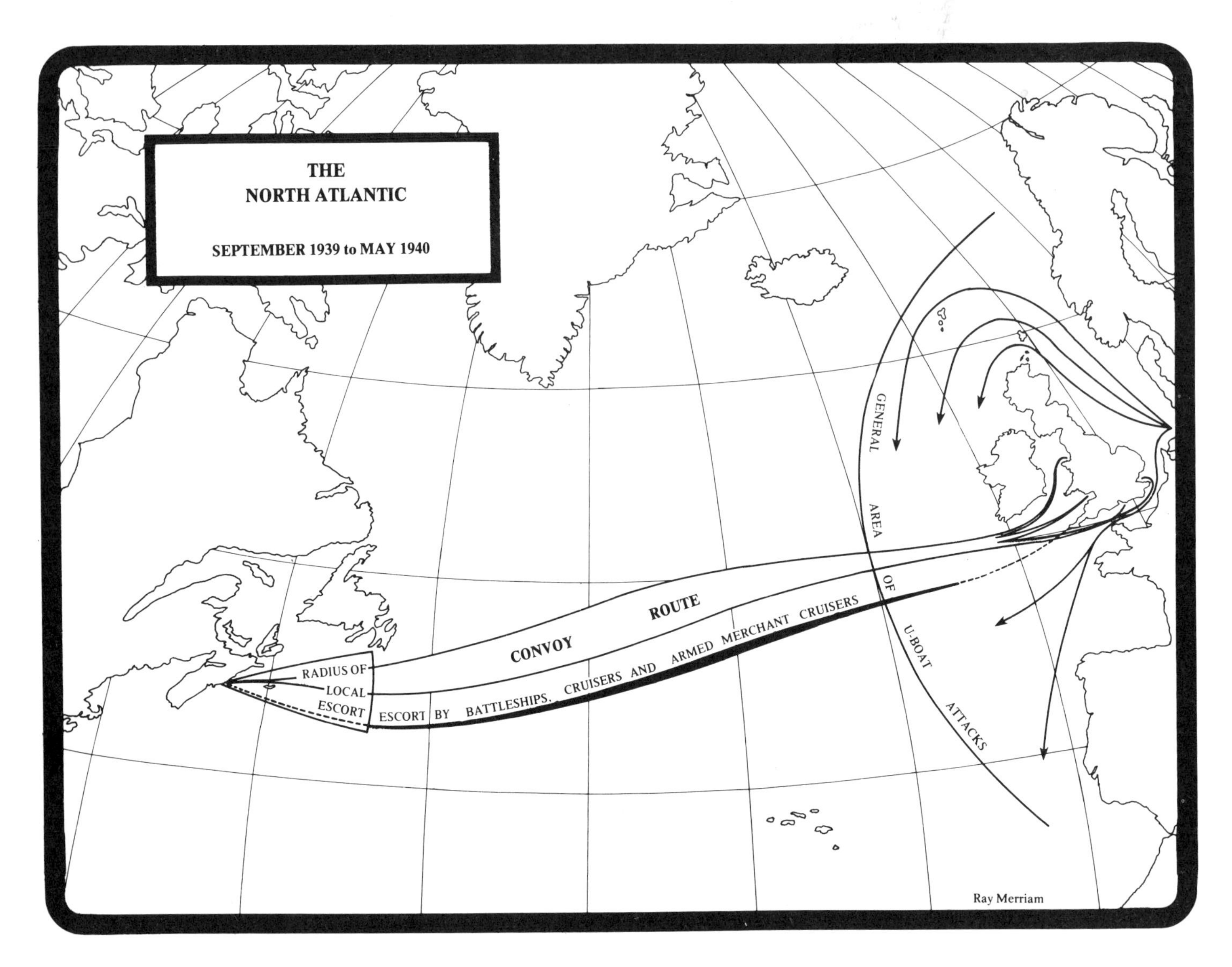

HMCS ARNPRIOR, one of Canada's Castle Class corvettes at sea. C1 Escort Group green Maple Leaf shows on her stack. Sharp raked bow and squared stern, plus latticed mast are indicators of this class. Note open-topped bridge, 272 radar on platform mast, type 291 air warning aerial, and type 86 TBS aerials on cross-trees. Paint is light gray overall, with medium gray silhouette. [Ken MacPherson]

HMCS BELLEVILLE, October 1944, newly commissioned, prepares to visit her namesake town, Belleville, Ontario, on her way to the Atlantic. She sports a WA pattern of WA blue over white, but this would not last long in operational waters. Note the Canadian Red Ensign and the 'full dress' of signal flags." [Public Archives of Canada]

HMCS BOWMANVILLE the only Castle Class corvette to be based on the east coast at Digby, Nova Scotia. Note the dark gray hull, light gray upperworks, which was common in 1945 and would become the post-war coloration for the RCN. Note the 272 lantern has been moved to midpoint on the mast to make way for a more versatile Type 277 surface warning radar." [McBride collection, Maritime Museum of the Atlantic]

HMCS TILLSONBURG just clearing St. John's harbor (note Marconi's tower on top of bluff). She has the 272 radar on top of the mast and the Admiralty Disuptive scheme in light/dark gray. [Public Archives of Canada]

CALGARY, shown here in a Admiralty Disruptive pattern of 1943 vintage, but done in a three-tone coloration! Off-white, light grey and medium grey are used. Note the 291 air warning radar aerial at mast top, type 86 TBS antenna at cross-tree, 271P radar, and open-style bridge. Also the bandstand is in the forward Admiralty position. Probably 1944. [Author's collection]

ORILLA as she appeared in 1942, in a scruffy three-tone paint scheme. Note the monkey island on top of the compass house and the SW2CQ antenna at mast top. The Canadian SW1 and SW2 radars were good only when NOT needed. [Ken MacPherson]

day was quiet. Eight ships had been sunk so far and evening was coming on. The escort group was also smaller, as *Orillia* escorted *Tahchee* to Iceland. The attacks occurred all that night, making 48 hours without sleep for the escort vessels. Only one ship was sunk, before the escort force was reinforced by two corvettes, *Moose Jaw* and *Chambly*, who had been exercising their new crews off Greenland and had obtained permission to relieve the escorts of SC-42. Commander J. D. Prentice had driven his crews hard for the past two weeks and now the training was going to pay off. His comment to his 'Jimmy on One' enroute was to prove prophetic: "When we get there we'll not have to worry about the convoy. Our job will be to find the enemy and kill him."

They arrived on 10 September, at dusk. They sighted the flares of a stricken ship and proceeded towards that position. *Moose Jaw* was on *Chambly*'s starboard side. Eighteen minutes later, *Chambly* obtained an Asdic contact. She tracked the contact for two minutes and then laid a pattern of depth charges. The U-boat surged to the surface, about 400 yards off *Moose Jaw*'s port bow and proceeded to run across her bows. *Moose Jaw* opened fire and increased her speed, bearing down on the U-boat. The sub stopped engines and abandoned its attempt to run. The corvette ran in alongside, with the German crew mostly on deck, with their hands in the air. The U-boat captain stepped from the "cigarette deck" to the deck of *Moose Jaw*, without even wetting his feet. The corvette sheared off to prevent further boardings and as the stern swung around, the hidden part of the U-boat crew attempted to get her underway again. However, as *Moose Jaw* swung back, they attempted to cross her bows — a fatal mistake. *Moose Jaw* promptly rammed and then shelled the crew trying to man the deck

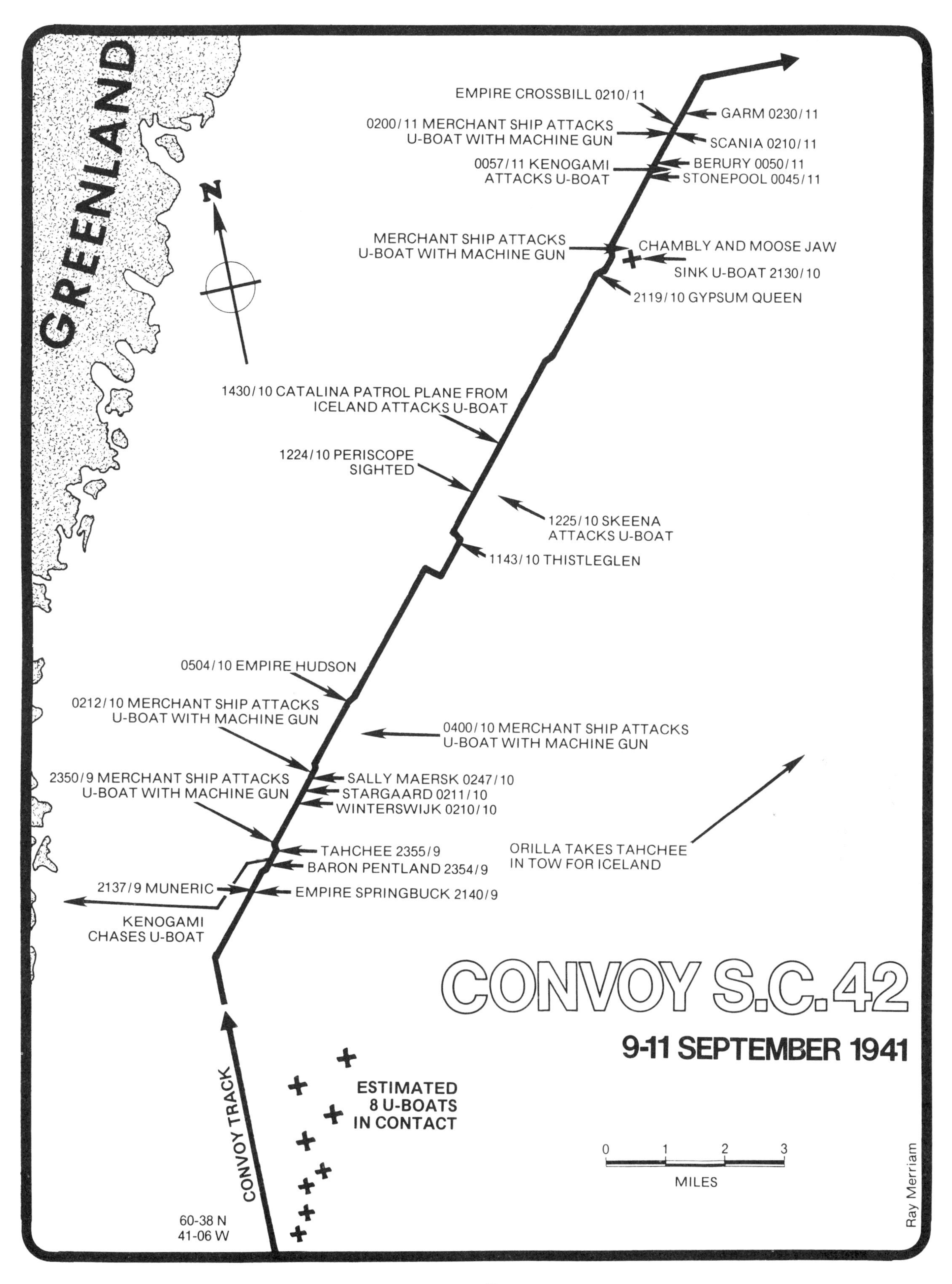
GREENLAND
N
EMPIRE CROSSBILL 0210/11
GARM 0230/11
0200/11 MERCHANT SHIP ATTACKS
U-BOAT WITH MACHINE GUN
SCANIA 0210/11
0057/11 KENOGAMI
ATTACKS U-BOAT
BERURY 0050/11
STONEPOOL 0045/11
MERCHANT SHIP ATTACKS
U-BOAT WITH MACHINE GUN
CHAMBLY AND MOOSE JAW
SINK U-BOAT 2130/10
2119/10 GYPSUM QUEEN
1430/10 CATALINA PATROL PLANE FROM
ICELAND ATTACKS U-BOAT
1224/10 PERISCOPE
SIGHTED
1225/10 SKEENA
ATTACKS U-BOAT
1143/10 THISTLEGLEN
0504/10 EMPIRE HUDSON
0212/10 MERCHANT SHIP ATTACKS
U-BOAT WITH MACHINE GUN
0400/10 MERCHANT SHIP ATTACKS
U-BOAT WITH MACHINE GUN
2350/9 MERCHANT SHIP ATTACKS
U-BOAT WITH MACHINE GUN
SALLY MAERSK 0247/10
STARGAARD 0211/10
WINTERSWIJK 0210/10
TAHCHEE 2355/9
BARON PENTLAND 2354/9
ORILLA TAKES TAHCHEE
IN TOW FOR ICELAND
2137/9 MUNERIC
EMPIRE SPRINGBUCK 2140/9
KENOGAMI
CHASES U-BOAT
CONVOY S.C.42
9-11 SEPTEMBER 1941
CONVOY TRACK
ESTIMATED
8 U-BOATS
IN CONTACT
0
1
2
3
MILES
60-38 N
41-06 W
Ray Merriam

gun.

Chambly came alongside and put a boarding party aboard under Lt. Edward T. Simmons, who ordered the remaining 11 crew on the casing below. They refused, at pistol point, which indicated the U-boat was being scuttled. The boarding party boiled below to try to salvage the U-boat, finding all the gauges smashed, as well as the lighting. The outrushing air gave grim notice of the water coming in below. With a sudden lurch, the sub began to settle. Stoker Bill I. Brown was sucked to his death within the hull as he attempted to leave. The remaining prize crew and all but 11 crew members were picked up. The U-boat captain insisted that the only reason he had surrendered was that so his crew would be spared. The Canadians remained suspicious, but eventually picked them up. U-501 had come to grief on her first operational trip to a pair of Canadian corvettes on *their* first operational sortie.

Chambly and *Moose Jaw* rejoined the convoy, where the battle still flared. At 2100 hours, two more ships were sunk and two more shortly after 0100 hours of the 11th. *Kenogami* sighted the U-boat, drove her under with gunfire and battered her with depth charges, without success. The sub was U-85, which was sunk nine months later by USS *Roper* and papers from the U-boat testified to the story.

MOOSE JAW is in a three-tone Western Approaches scheme, extra Carley floats are carried forward. Pennant number is in white, outlined in very thin black. Note the monkey house is of wood, and the building of such was accomplished by bribing dockyard workers with rum. [Public Archives of Canada]

HMCS CHAMBLY in a three-tone (off-white, WA green, WA blue) scheme. This is probably in 1944, as a hedgehog can be seen on the starboard foredeck, tucked up close to the bridge, as well as star rocket rails on the gun shield. She has the 291 A.W. (Air Warning) radar at mast top, a 252 IFF (Identification Friend or Foe) for 271 radar just below the mast head, and the last style bridge. [Marcom]

HMCS HALIFAX, taken 13 November 1941, shows the revised format of the 1940-1941 program. Lengthened forecastle and more rake and sheer at the bows for better seakeeping abilities. Note the canvas dodgers and same on the monkey island railings. Overall gray. [Public Archives of Canada]

Two more ships were torpedoed within a half hour and three more before dawn. A total of fifteen ships lost and one damaged. The exhausted corvettes and destroyer did their best to shield the convoy and fought on until 1200 hours of the 11th, when the welcome sight of British destroyers of the Western Approaches Escort Group were spotted. One more ship would be lost before the convoy reached Great Britain.

September in Greenland saw the first loss of a Canadian corvette. *Levis* was part of the escort of SC-44 and in the early hours of 19 September, a torpedo struck her forward on the port side, ripping the plating to within 40 feet of her stern and breaking her back under the crew's quarters. Seventeen men were killed. *Mayflower* came alongside and put a tow aboard, as *Levis* was upright and floating. She remained afloat for five hours and then listed to port and sank. Forty suvivors were taken off by *Mayflower* and *Agassiz.*

Another heavy battle developed around convoy SC-48, 400 miles south of Iceland on the morning of 15 October. The escort consisted of seven corvettes — five Canadian, one Free French, and one British — plus the Canadian four-stacker, *Columbia*, via Lease-Lend. She would act as the convoy commodore's vessel.

The first torpedo found the escort short three corvettes, who were busy astern

KENOGAMI in her earlier years, probably late 1941-early 1942. Note that she has the early main mast and Mark II minesweeping gear. What appears to be twin Lewis .303 machine guns are mounted in the bandstand. Overall medium gray. [Marcom]

rounding up stragglers. They were immediately recalled. At 2330 hours a second ship was torpedoed, and *Columbia* fired a star shell, which illuminated a third torpedoing. HMS *Gladiolus* set off to stalk the U-boat, but instead received a torpedo herself and sank with all hands just before dawn.

Four American destroyers arrived at 1300 hours on the 16th; later the British ships *Lobelia* and *Broadwater* joined the convoy. That night, six ships were lost, plus USS *Kearney*, which moved the United States one step closer to outright war. HMS *Veronica* and the Canadian corvette *Pictou* arrived on the scene about 2400 hours, and *Pictou* immediately gained a contact as she joined the convoy at about 0100 hours. She attacked, and a few moments later the U-boat's turbulance was seen dead ahead and rapidly drawing away. *Pictou* engaged by gunfire and received two near-misses by torpedoes in return. However, *Pictou* gained on the sub, which

HMCS MAYFLOWER lying off HMCS LEVIS, stopped after being torpedoed off Greenland, 19 September 1941. Both vessels medium gray. [Public Archives of Canada]

LEVIS, torpedoed, her bows broken, hull gashed open to the forepeak well, still floats. She remained that way for five hours. Note what appears to be two twin Vickers .303 machine guns in the bandstand, shrouded. [Public Archives of Canada]

alarmed the U-boat captain, who then made a mistake: he suddenly sheared off to starboard and presented a silhouette. *Pictou* tried to ram, but the U-boat swung to port, and then *Pictou* showed her whaler design — she cut inside the U-boat's circle! The U-boat attempted to crash-dive at 100 yards' distance and just made it under. *Pictou* dropped a varied depth charge pattern into the still-boiling waters over the U-boat. The resultant explosions were followed by a huge air bubble, fifteen feet high. A 'probable damaged' for the *Pictou*.

In October and November there were signs that this inadequately equipped force was having some effect. Germany had five times the number of U-boats at sea in September 1941 as they had had one year before, yet the total tonnage sunk had dropped off by 50,000 tons that month. U-boats were now more cautious, fired from longer distances, and received more punishment. The ratio of U-boats sunk versus ships sunk had risen to 1:10, and

Close-up of damage to LEVIS. Charred area was from fire of paint stores where torpedo hit. [Marcom]

One in a series of depth charges going off behind an unidentified corvette. [Marcom]

the building programs were building two merchantmen for every one sunk.

Winter closed in with its usual grimness, and now the convoys spent two-thirds of their trip in Arctic darkness. The chances of survival, if torpedoed, were very slim. The cold of the water, lack of lifesaving gear and vessels all stacked up to make life grim.

As the ships plowed on in the Arctic gales, sleet and spray froze to every piece of metal, glass, rope, and clothes. The crews spent considerable time beating foot-thick ice off the ship's upper works with fire axes, to keep the ship from turning turtle from the excessive weight. Some large merchant vessels were lost this way, as the ice built up faster than the crew could remove it.

Three days out of St. John's the bread was a mass of mold; fresh meat and vegetables perished in the wringing wet. Hard tack and pickled beef, in tins, plus lime juice became the staples, as in Nelson's time.

Unwashed, unshaven, freezing at their posts, soaking wet below decks, as water shipped through every hatchway and ventilator and the bulkheads streamed with condensation, the crews carried on with their duties. Gales battered the ships, to be followed by huge swells called 'milestones' which hammered the ships and rattled the teeth in the seamens' heads. Seasickness was no excuse; it did not exist, according to shore-

HMCS PICTOU in 1944, with dark gray lower hull, light gray upper hull and superstructure. Whaler racing while awaiting the cross-Channel invasion. [Marcom]

Unidentified corvette, looking aft on the quarterdeck, shows how salt water ice could build up. [Public Archives of Canada]

BRANTFORD, looking at the 4-inch mount, bridge in the background. Icing like this was common throughout the winter months of the war. St. John's, Newfoundland, 22 February 1944. Note the condition of the seaman; everyone looked this way. Type 271 radar lantern in background. [Public Archives of Canada]

side medical officers (M.O.'s). Men lived on soup and fruit juice for the entire voyage, but they did their job. After Greenland, the leg to Iceland, with its lack of facilities for crews, lack of fresh provisions, and lack of warmth in the women. Fueling, repairs, and landing wounded and survivors, plus all the sleep you could manage were the main activities. Then supposedly 48 hours lay-over (usually much less, like five hours, because you were late arriving). Later the escort of the westbound convoy that was leaving British waters. The monotony was tremendous and the rest periods were non-existant. The Royal Canadian Navy was stretched to her limits.

Alan Easton wrote about one of these convoys, and after the ship had reached the eastern meeting point, that this occurred:

"Once, in the 56 hours after a first ship had been torpedoed, in one convoy, my snatches of sleep totaled about three and a half hours. Perhaps it was not surprising then, as we straightened away with the job over, that I could speak, coherently, only about half a sentence as I tried to give the navigator my final instructions. My words would dwindle into nonsense. I struggled against this and by standing erect and moving about a little on the bridge, I thought I eventually conveyed my wishes to him. Then I went below and collapsed into my bunk.

"Two years later I met the navigator and asked, 'Do you remember when we turned north to Reyjavik after that action? It was a bit after lunch and I was going to turn in.'

"'Yes,' he answered. 'I remember turning north and taking over.'

"'Do you know,' I said, 'I was so tired I was falling asleep as I was speaking to you. I felt embarrassed in case you noticed it. Did you?'

"'Did I?' A broad grin. 'No, sir. I was too sleepy to know what you were talking about!'"

Always fuel was a problem. With diversions to avoid U-boats and bad weather, many ships watched the last few tons of oil like misers over their money. Occasionally, with tanks empty, they lay hove-to, awaiting a tow, vulnerable to subs and powerless to fight a storm.

Ships bulged and bristled with more and better armament and equipment. This also meant more men to man it, which meant overcrowding of already sardine tin-like accomodations. Men slept on decks, *in* lockers, in hammocks, at the foot of companionways — anywhere they could find

Even corvettes were not immune to damage in heavy North Atlantic storms. Frozen spray has effectively covered most fittings on the forepeak, and the foremast has snapped off and fallen across the gunshield of the 4 inch. This was unusual, probably caused by a sudden whipping action coming off a wave top, plus fatigue in the mast. [Maritime Museum of the Atlantic]

MATAPEDIA charges out of the fog, sometime in 1944. Note the port offset 271, plus extended bridge with Asdic hut overhanging the bridge face. Two color camouflage scheme. [Marcom]

Photo shows great detail of depth charge throwers, dan buoys, and superstructure during a bit of dirty weather. Note the one-piece oilskin and sou'wester on the deck hand. 1941. [Marcom]

space to lie down. The typical crew's mess was 22 feet by 32 feet and contained sixty men. Rooms were pie-shaped with above widest measurements.

By December 1941, sixty-four corvettes were in commission, with sixty more ordered for 1942-43.

The storms of 1941-42 were some of the worst ever experienced in modern times. They hindered ships and U-boats alike, with seven successive convoys, westward-bound, being dispersed by huge waves and continuous storms. One storm and ship summed up the whole thing with HMCS *Baddeck*:

> "...one dark night, making for port after leaving the convoy, and running before the high, quarterly sea, the ship was pitching and rolling deeply, slowly — too slowly. The waves almost synchronized with her speed. At times she rode like a surfboat before the rollers with her nose pointing down.
>
> "At 2045 [hours], the stern rose high and the ship rolled 50 degrees to port and hung for an interminable time until the great sea relented and plowed forward along the keel. When the leading seaman of the watch was able to check several minutes later, the aft lookout man was not on the high gun platform. The bulwarks on the starboard quarter were bent inboard, the protective plating on the gun platform almost flattened and the large raft on the port side gone — damage that told that the lookout had been swept overboard. The great sea must have buried the whole after end of the ship. We turned to search, but as we rose and dived into the steep seas we knew we could never find him. His close friend and shipmate cried for days and nights."

In the lulls between the storms, blinding fog added to the dangers. These conditions led to the loss of the corvette *Windflower*

MIDLAND, 1942, with a dark dark gray/light gray Western Approaches pattern. Note the SW2CQ antenna at mast top. [Marcom]

HMCS SACKVILLE, an interesting shot showing a .303 water-jacketed machine gun in the bandstand and the Mark II gear still aboard. In 1942 early Western Approaches paint. SW2CQ Yagi antenna at mast head. Note deterioration of paint from weather and rust, this camouflage's worst enemy. [Ken MacPherson]

HMCS SPIKENARD, sporting a very neat three-tone Western Approaches. Note the splinter mats on bridge railings, wood monkey island, SW2CQ antenna. Probably just after refit, autumn, 1941. [Public Archives of Canada]

on 7 December 1941, under command of Lt. J. Price. *Windflower* was rammed by the freighter *Zypenburg* in dense fog. One of the ship's boilers exploded, cooking a large part of the crew in their berths. Ten minutes later she sank by the stern, leaving 47 survivors, three of whom later died, to be picked up by *Nasturtium* and *Zypenburg*. Thus ended the short life of this plucky ship exactly eleven months after she had arrived in Britain with her wooden gun.

After 7 December 1941 and Pearl Harbor, all the elaborate plans of the three countries' navies fell apart. Three U.S. battleships, three cruisers, an aircraft carrier, and two squadrons of destroyers had been transferred to the Atlantic in May were now recalled. In July, U.S. forces had relieved the British forces in Ireland. Then in August the Atlantic Charter had been signed, and the Atlantic had been divided east and west, and the American Navy took over the strategic control of the western half. Still at 'peace', the U.S. was determined that their enormous tonnages of war material sold to Britain should get through. The U.S. Navy and air forces would be responsible to the 30th Meridian West, roughly off Iceland. A large base at Argentia, in Newfoundland, a concession gained in the Lease-Lend Agreement, and authority in the Western Atlantic devolved to the American admiral there. The first 'HX' convoy under American escort sailed on 16 September 1941, and all 'HX' convoys were planned to be so from then on. 'SC' con-

ARVIDA, coming alongside a Senior Escort to receive something. Very prominent is the SW2CQ antenna, her three-tone paint, and her striped funnel band, which indicates the C5 Escort Group, the "Barber Pole Brigade". Winter of 1942. [Marcom]

DAUPHIN, 1941. Note the mainmast and gaff not removed, wooden planking on foredeck, Mark II minesweeping gear. The Vickers 2-pounder is not fitted, although it is hard to see the two .303 machine guns in the bandstand. Overall medium gray with early Disruptive pattern. Only gun-shield and bows have been done. [Marcom]

voys from Sydney were under Canadian control, until off Iceland, where all escort duties would become British.

The American commander-in-chief in Argentia was one Adm. Bristol, and he and Commodore Murray at St. John's were realists and could cooperate in staff duties. Thus the U.S. forces would relieve the pressure that the RCN was laboring under up until that time.

However, this all came tumbling down with 7 December 1941 and Pearl Harbor. Before the American presence in the Atlantic theatre could be felt, it had to be withdrawn to cover America's Pacific Coast. Even worse, this now reduced the number of British units, as Britian now had another ocean to patrol. *Prince of Wales* and *Repulse* had been sunk on 9 December 1941 and the slack had to be taken up by smaller units — destroyers, that is.

LETHBRIDGE, in 1944. Note the Light Admiralty Disruptive in dark gray and offwhite. She has the 291-type antenna, but with the SW2C set, 271P radar, and expanded bridge with 20mm Oerlikons. Note the depth charge rails appear to have been removed. [Marcom]

By February 1942 only two Coast Guard cutters remained on escort duty in the Atlantic. The Canadian Navy had to take up the duties in the Western Atlantic, which again stretched the RCN to the limit and nearly broke it.

Ships of the Local Escort Force, operating between Halifax, Sydney, and St. John's had a short trip, but because of the fog and foul weather it was one of the most dangerous areas in the North Atlantic. Mid-ocean groups (St. John's to Iceland) were supposed to have twelve days in harbor for every 24 days spent at sea. However, this was rarely the case, with heavy weather delays and detours because of sightings. When they rendezvoused with the British escorts, they still had 24 hours of steaming to reach Iceland to refuel. Casualties, repairs, etc., they all had to be done, and often it was that a escort sailed within 48 hours of arrival! Twelve to fourteen days saw them back off St. John's, only to be ordered to Halifax for refit or because St. John's harbor was too crowded. Despite the added four day journey, the escorts had to be ready for the next east-bound convoy! This resulted in great strain and the groups were constantly undermanned. Men carried on after a fashion, but machines broke down, and the numbers of escorts out of service through enemy action or mechanical breakdown increased alarmingly. The entire fabric of the Western Atlantic Escort System was falling apart.

The situation was being watched intently by the British, American, and Canadian officials, but not much could be done to relieve the situation. Still under the Atlantic Charter, Canada had to accept responsibility of the fast 'independents', as the American refused to do so. A Diversion room was set up in Naval Headquarters (N.H.Q.), Halifax, to handle this.

The withdrawal of American warships brought the entire matter of strategic control by Americans under debate. Since the warships were Canadian and British, this arrangement was becoming complicated, but for now nothing could be done.

The reorganization came in February 1942. It affected mainly Canadian ships which formed the main strength of the Western Sector Escorts, with thirteen destroyers and seventy corvettes. The Western Local Escort Force (Halifax to Newfoundland) had their western terminus extended out to sea from Halifax by 700 miles (45 degrees West). The Newfoundland Escort Force (Newfoundland to Iceland) had their eastern terminus changed to Londonderry, Northern Ireland, instead of Iceland. This would mean a longer layover than before, and the number of escorts per convoy was decreased from seven to six.

Convoy SC 67 in February 1942 was the first to use this new system. The Mid-Ocean Groups started the famous 'Newfie to Derry' runs, of which they would see plenty for the next three years.

One of the corvettes of SC 67 was destined never to see the Foyle of Ireland. *Spikenard*, the senior escort (Lt. Cdr. H. G. Shadforth) was lost on the night of 10 February 1942. The convoy had started in fog and then encountered heavy weather until south of Iceland, without a U-boat attack. Shortly before 2300 hours, the tanker *Heina* was torpedoed. *Spikenard* was on the starboard quarter and quite close. At the same time, another torpedo struck *Spikenard*, the nearest other corvette being *Chilliwack* (Lt. L. F. Foxall, RCNR) who was engaged with an Asdic contact when *Spikenard* was hit. Mountainous seas hid the truth from *Chilliwack*, who believed that only one vessel had been torpedoed.*Dauphin* (Lt. R. A. S. McNeil) astern of the convoy, starboard side, and three miles distant, saw two explosions, and set off for the *Heina*, which was now ablaze. She found the tanker settling by the head. She immediately lowered nets and spent the next two hours picking up survivors.

Shediac (Lt. John E. Clayton, RCNR) had observed the torpedoing from the port rear quarter at seven miles, came alongside of *Dauphin* and was ordered to search for a second torpedoed ship.

Louisburg (Lt. Cdr. W. F. Campbell) had been nearest *Spikenard*, about 1¼ miles astern, but she had been dodging torpedoes on her port side. She had turned and followed their tracks, gained a contact, and attacked for 1½ hours.

Lethbridge (Lt. H. Freeland, RCNR) was several miles away, on the port quarter. She had seen and heard heavy explosions across the convoy, and seen the explosion of *Heina*, but did not leave her station. Throughout the night each tried to raise *Spikenard*, but it was written off to equipment failure and no great concern was felt. Wireless

SUDBURY, late 1944, with 271 radar offset to port, 291 air warning radar, and three-tone 1943 Western Approaches paint scheme. [Public Archives of Canada]

silence was to be maintained, so further contact was not attempted. However, dawn brought the grim truth, but still she could have been hull-down over the horizon. By 1100 hours the British escorts had appeared and the corvette *Gentian* was sent to conduct a search. After seven hours of hunting she came across a Carley float with eight survivors, all that were ever found.

The survivors, none of which were bridge crew, remembered action stations had been sounded and speed had increased, then the torpedoes struck. In *Spikenard*, impact had occurred between bridge and forecastle, tearing part of the ship's side and deck away. Fire immediately broke out, destroying the bridge, wireless office, and the boats on that side. Gasoline stored in drums below the bridge, lashed to the mast, exploded, engulfed the superstructure and flowed in fiery streams through holes into the interior of the ship. Men had to fight their way up hatchways, through the flames, with some falling into the flooded forepeak, through the gaping hole in the maindeck as they gained it. *Spikenard* began to settle by the head, with the steam whistle screaming her death cry, she sank in less than five minutes. As the sea covered her, an enormous explosion, either her boilers or depth charges, smashed the remaining boat and one Carley float. She disappeared entirely before *Dauphin* reached her area, and their attention was drawn by the flaming *Heina.*

The loss of *Spikenard* was nearly ignored to all other than next of kin with the shocking news of 12 February 1942 of the loss of the British ship *Cyclops* just 160 miles south of Halifax. This sinking presaged the coming of some twenty U-boats to the waters of the American seaboard. The "happy time" of the U-boats was about to begin.

From Hatteras to Newfoundland the blow fell heavy. During the nineteen subsequent days of February, 39 ships for a total tonnage of 250,000 were sunk; sixteen of these were tankers and were sunk in shallow waters, showing the scorn that the U-boat commanders had for American anti-submarine strategy. During the following month, watchers from Key West to Boston watched in horror as more than two hundred merchantmen and tankers were sunk, all within ten miles of shore!

These attacks, which annoyed the United States, was becoming a stranglehold on Britain's oil supplies. Oil from the Far East had dried up with the conquests by the Japanese. Middle East oil was nearly cut off in the Mediterranean, and Persian Gulf oil was threatened in the Indian Ocean by Japanese raiders and submarines. The remaining fuel and lubricants came from Aruba, Curacao, and the Gulfs of Mexico and Venezuela, and now the U-boats threatened to cut this off. The total sunk by U-boats for January/February reached 144 ships of nearly 800,000 tons and the carnage continued. Without convoy-type protection (which Adm. King, USN, refused to do) the oil stocks of the United Kingdom, Canada, and the United States fell to dangerous levels.

March saw the U-boat attacks swing back north, between Charleston and New York, and Cape Hatteras became a ships' graveyard, with as many as six ships a night being sunk. U-boats preyed on unescorted vessels, ignoring any makeshift convoys completely, to avoid any damage to themselves from escort action. They made every torpedo count and when all were expended, they engaged with deck guns, often within scant miles of shore.

The first remedial actions were the formation of the 'BX' and 'XB' convoys between Boston and Halifax. These were escorted by Canadian units withdrawn from the Western Local Escort Force, which diluted this organization further. They assembled in Buzzard's Bay, south of Cape Cod Bay, and proceeded to Cape Cod Bay to escort their convoy to Halifax. The first of these sailed on 20 March and this proved to spell the end of the easy pickings that the U-boats had enjoyed between Boston and Halifax. However, points south of Boston were still unescorted and the slaughter carried on there for several months to come.

In March 1942, meetings were held and revisions made of the existing convoy plans from Quebec City to Sydney. A Gaspe base for Gulf Escort Forces was proposed, but with the over-extension of the Local Escort Force and weakening of the Mid-Ocean Group to cover the Boston-Halifax convoys, the plan remained a paper proposal, until the arrival of U-boats in the St. Lawrence in mid-June.

The arrival of U-553 and her spectacular sinkings between 11-12 June, touched off a near-panic in Ottawa. The only forces in the Gulf of St. Lawrence were a Bangor class minesweeper and two gas-powered M.G.B. Fairmiles, which fruitlessly searched for the U-boat. They were later joined by five more Bangors, withdrawn from the

COBURG, again in 1944, but wearing a two-color paint scheme of light gray/medium green. Note star rocket rails and storage lockers. [Ken MacPherson]

A beautiful shot of SHEDIAC, shot on 16 December 1944. The paint is off-white with medium gray false hull. The pennant numbers are odd in being so bold. Note the hedgehog on the starboard side, aft of the 4-inch mount. Also all the anti-aircraft weapons are shrouded. Artwork on gunshield is old tomcat with Canadian sailors' cap on, hunting a U-boat fish in a goldfish bowl. These will be presented in a later publication. [Marcom]

Western Escort Force and the delayed Gaspe base was activated, as well as the revised Quebec City-Sydney convoys. But the Navy steadfastly refused to withdraw further units from the hard-pressed Escort Force (West). The U-boat attacks were to be officially quashed, and played-down. Ten days later, U-553 left the St. Lawrence, still under wireless silence (unusual for the methodical U-boat procedure of once-daily reports).

The U-boats, for reasons unknown then, switched back to the Atlantic routes. On 11-12 May, there were repeated attacks on a convoy escorted by the Canadian corvettes *Bittersweet, Algoma, Shediac,* and *Arvida,* plus two American destroyers. Four U-boats sank six merchantmen in very short order and retired, leaving the escorts to pick up the survivors (about 2200 hours). The tracking resumed the next night and in desperation the convoy took evasive action at 2359 hours. As the order was being executed, a panicky ship fired 'snowflake' to illuminate a suspected U-boat and other ships followed suit, turning night into day and betraying the convoy's position. A ship was torpedoed and in the confusion *Arvida* was fired upon by an armed merchantman. The convoy was then abandoned by the U-boats.

June was worse than May, with 671,000 tons of shipping sent to the bottom off the American coast and in the Caribbean. Partial convoys and bucket-brigade escorts were finally allowed by the recalcitrant Adm. King, but still huge gaps existed, because of warship shortages. Tension became so great that the antiquated British sub, *P-514,* which was used for training exercises, was rammed and sunk with all hands by the Bangor class minesweeper, *Georgian,* when she ignored an Aldis lamp challenge.

U-boats in June laid mines in American harbor waters and landed saboteurs in Florida and on Long Island. All were captured. Five ships were lost to the mines. Panic in America was slowly pressuring the U.S. Navy into building up the Atlantic escorts, but the Pacific still had priority.

On 6 July 1942, three ships in convoy were torpedoed off Cap Chat and another off Cap de la Madeleine on the north shore of the St. Lawrence on the 20 July. The war had returned to Canada.

On 27 August, *U-517*, under Lt. Cdr. Paul Hartwig, sank the transport *Chatham* in the Strait of Belle Isle, off Cape Bauld. He evaded the escorts and headed north, where he decided to proceed down the other side of the Strait. He and *U-165* attacked the same convoy and sank one ship apiece. On 3 September at 0130 hours, *U-517* torpedoed the *Donald Stewart* and dived to evade the corvette *Weyburn*. *Weyburn*'s depth charge throwers jammed and only two charges were gotten away. Needless to say, the attack was a failure. With the layering of fresh and salt water in the Gulf, contact was not regained.

On 4 September air attacks were made on *U-517*, with her being hit by a 500 pound bomb, which failed to explode. After evading the aircraft, *U-517* surfaced to find the bomb wedged between the pressure hull and the outer casing. The captain, engineering officer, and two ratings extracted the bomb and rolled it over the side. Hartwig's luck was still holding.

On 6 September, *U-517* was within 250 miles of Quebec City and stalking a convoy escorted by two corvettes, two Fairmiles, and an armed yacht *Raccoon*. *Arrowhead*, one of the corvettes, spotted the sub and Hartwig and his crew received their first real pounding. Lighting was knocked out, fittings sprung, and most glass was broken, when Hartwig deployed the newest anti-escort device, a perforated metal cylinder about eight inches in size. It was called 'Pillenwerfer', a chemical echo-maker which deceived the *Arrowhead*'s Asdic operator and while she attacked the decoy, *U-517* slipped away. The disappointed escorts rejoined the convoy and spent until 2359 hours picking up survivors. Two heavy detonations and the disappearance of the yacht *Raccoon* were unexplained. Only a body of a man from her crew was found, washed up on Anticosti Island, several days later.

At about 0430 hours on 8 September, *U-517* attacked the same convoy and sank three more ships and although the escorts gave him a hard time, he escaped, thanks to the layering effect of salt and fresh waters distorting the Asdic beams.

The 11th saw *U-517* off Gaspe again, and she attacked the corvette *Charlottetown* and the minesweeper *Clayoquot*. She was undetected and put two torpedoes into *Charlottetown* who, making 15 knots, started to drive herself under. She sank by the bows in three minutes and, as usual, the depth charges exploded, even although set on "safe", which killed six men and injured seven others. *Clayoquot* rescued 55, after vainly searching for the U-boat.

On the 15th and 16th, *U-165* and *U-517* attacked another Quebec-Sydney convoy, sinking two ships on the night of the 15th, and two more, by *U-165*, the morning of the 16th. Depth charge attacks only shook *U-517*, as Asdic performance was dismal. But the Canadian escorts had done damage. *U-517*'s firing gear was damaged and the distillers were reduced to 10 gallons per day, a severe loss. Hartwig had four torpedoes and a thirsty crew, as well as doubtful means to fire the former. He decided on one more go.

He attacked a convoy on 4 October and fired his last four torpedoes, which proceeded to run everywhere but where they were intended. Hartwig conceded defeat and slipped out of the Cabot Strait on 5 October on the way home. He had sunk a total of 31,101 tons of shipping, Allied ships and planes had dropped 27 bombs and 118 depth charges to very little avail. He was sunk, eventually, off Cape Ortegal, by a seaborne British plane in October, and Hartwig was captured by the British, afterwards revealing his part in the St. Lawrence action.

In June 1942, the Japanese occupied Attu and Kiska, off Alaska, which sparked American and Canadian forces in the Pacific Northwest. The merchant cruisers *Prince Robert*, *Henry* and *David*, with the corvettes *Dawson* and *Vancouver*, sailed to Kodiak, Alaska, on 20 August. They were to escort convoys between Kodiak, Dutch Harbor, and intermediate points, but saw no actual

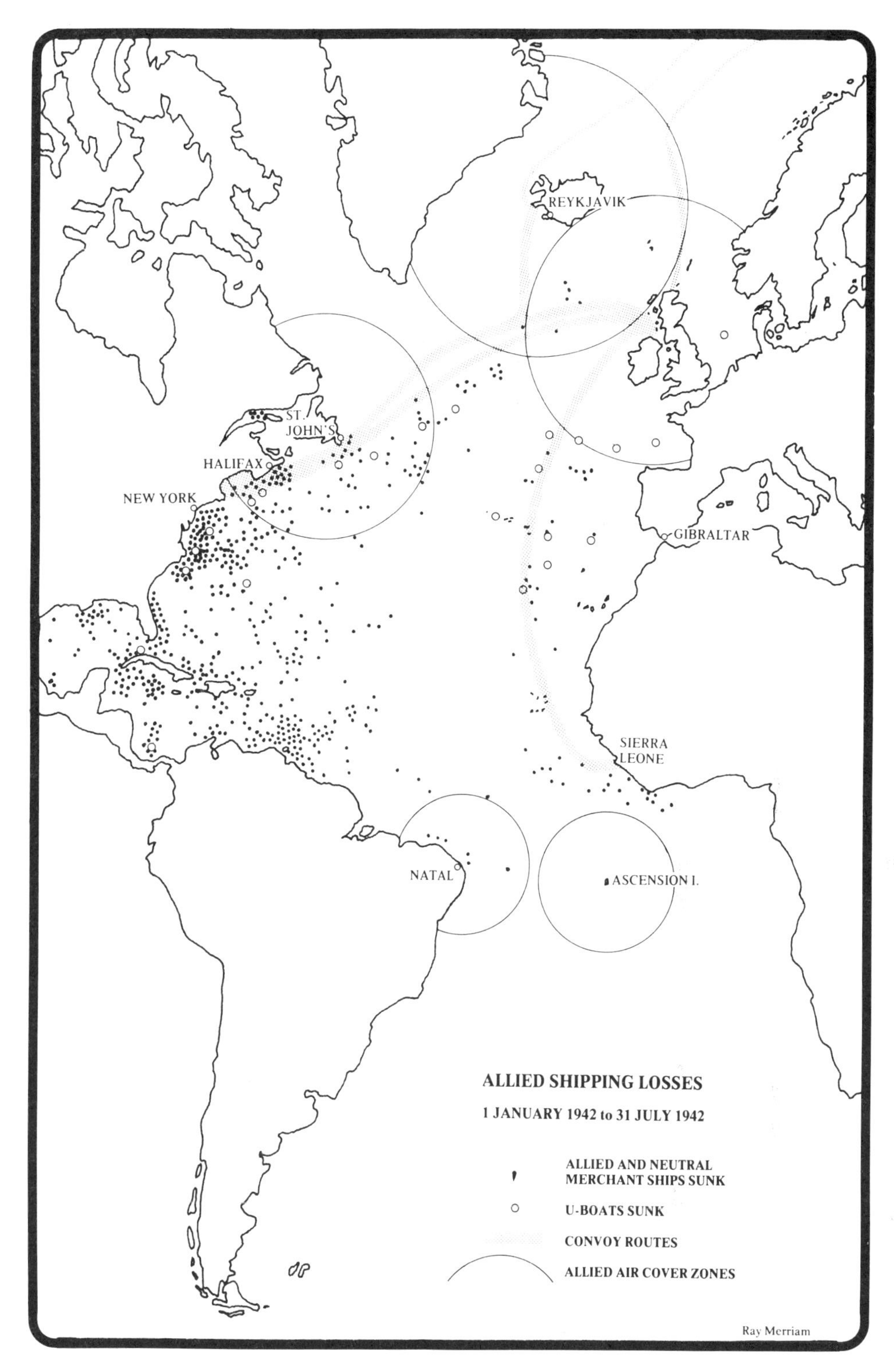

ALGOMA, sometime in 1942; note how the three-tone paint has pealed off in great swatches. Poor quality paint, plus the excessive humidity and salt build-up wore paint off rapidly. She still retains her mainmast. This is probably in Iceland. [Author's collection]

ALGOMA, in 1944, at Quebec City. Note at this late date she still has her forecastle. She has a two-tone paint scheme, with extra 20 mm Oerlikons aft. Note the triac stay from the foremast. [Marcom]

ARROWHEAD, sometime in 1942. She has a three-tone Western Approaches paint, but the interesting thing is the SQUARE radar housing on the bridge. Also a SW1 'bedspring' antenna on the mast; undoubtedly the most useless radar set of the war. Bridge has been widened but 20 mm are not yet fitted. Crest is an Indian head. [Marcom]

CHARLOTTETOWN, six months before her sinking, 11 September, off Gaspe. She was photographed here in March, in Halifax, off George's Island (background). She appears to be in a modified Peter Scott (1941) pattern, but only on her superstructure. The hull appears medium gray, with light gray overtones. Bandstand contains two machine guns. [Ken MacPherson]

CHARLOTTETOWN again, as she appeared in late summer of 1942, prior to being sunk. Full-fledged Western Approaches paint scheme has prevailed, as well as a two-pounder in the bandstand. See the of white blistering already. [Marcom]

DAWSON, one of the west coast-built corvettes and served in Canadian Pacific waters. One of the escorts slated for the Attu landings in the Alaskan Aleutians. This is in 1944-1945. Note the Admiralty Disruptive style paint scheme of medium grey over off-white. [Marcom]

HMCS VANCOUVER. Another Western-built corvette. Note she is hedgehog-equipped, has all modern radar, and star rocket rails. She is shown here escorting convoys in waters off the east coast. Note the pennant numbers done in black relief. Also, she is being refueled at sea, which was pretty standard by 1944-1945. [Marcom]

combat with Japanese forces, who soon withdrew.

1942: THE DEFENSES OF CANADA

Thirteen destroyers, 68 corvettes, 20 Bangors, and 60 smaller craft were devoted to the defense of convoy routes from the Caribbean to Ireland, and now had importance all out of context because of the vital nature of their work. United States forces in the Atlantic were limited to Coast Guard vessels, being occupied in the Pacific theatre to a major extent. Great Britain's capital ships held the gates of the North Sea, Indian Ocean, and the South Atlantic, leaving destroyers, corvettes, etc., in British waters to guard the Eastern Atlantic Approaches for Britain's vital convoys.

The Battle of the Atlantic would be fought with these little ships that the Regular Navy had scorned, awaiting the big ships to conduct the second Battle of Jutland. Modern destroyers were wasted plodding along with these slow convoys. The old four-stackers of Lease-Lend, plus the corvettes were the economical answer. This would be Canada's contribution to the sea war. By mid-1942, 40% of escort work of convoys in the North Atlantic was being done by Canadians. This was recognized and accepted as Canada's role by Canadian authorities. By the end of the summer of 1942, Canadian escorts had escorted 65 million tons of cargo to Britain, when the main sailing point on the western end was changed to New York. Canadian ships with their half-trained crews, still too few and far between, with antiquated ships and equipment and not enough of that, had made it possible for

ST. CLAIR, one of our old four-stackers that were obtained from the United States under Lease-Lend. She is shown here with 271 radar, her third stack sealed off, 291 air warning radar, and Western Approaches three-tone paint. [McBride Collection, Maritime Museum of the Atlantic]

this cargo to get through to Britain at this critical time.

On 31 July 1942, the destroyer *Skeena* (with this author's father aboard) and the corvette *Wetaskiwin*, participated in a documented battle with a U-boat. At this time there had grown a cult or craze of using Biblical verses to convey messages to other ships. Thus a New Testament, plus a Concordance was necessary equipment on any bridge.

Seven hundred miles off Newfoundland, *Skeena* was depth charging a doubtful contact, when *Wetaskiwin* hove over the horizon. *Skeena* signalled the corvette for assistance with the signal, "Act 16, verse 9". Out came the Bible on *Wetaskiwin*'s bridge, thus read the passage, "And a vision appeared to Paul in the night; there stood a man of Macedonia and prayed him saying, come over into Macedonia and help us".

Hurriedly, the corvette's crew whipped out the Concordance and sent the following: "Revelations 13, Verse 1". Now it was *Skeena*'s turn to look it up. It read: "And I stood upon the sand of the sea and saw a beast rise up out of the sea having seven heads and ten horns, and upon his horns ten crowns, and upon his head the name of blasphemy". Which, although not the most appropriate, was pretty good for that short period of time. Apparently the Lord did not have his ears open, for it took five hours further to sink the U-boat. *Skeena* and *Wetaskiwin* entered the ranks of those who had hit back with some result.

The convoy that *Skeena* and *Wetaskiwin* were helping to protect (both were members of C3 Escort Group) was one of the ones that the U-boat screen picked up, intercepted and formed a pack on. The corvette *Sackville* sighted a U-boat at dusk on 31 July, and raced to contact her. However, the appearance of 'snowflake' indicated a

A Mark II depth charge thrower cuts loose, watched by its crew. Note the stem support does NOT detach, which was corrected in the Mark IV to save metal in England. Most Canadian corvettes used the Mark IV, as it was available. HMCS PICTOU, March 1942. Note twin .303 machine guns in bandstand. [Public Archives of Canada]

A 1940-1941 photo of WETASKIWIN, known as the 'Wet Ass Queen' to friends. Note the mainmast, Mark II minesweeping gear, and short fo'c's'le, plus nothing in the bandstand. Canvas dodgers show to good advantage. [Public Archives of Canada]

SACKVILLE, undergoing builder's anchor trials, December 1941, Halifax harbour. Paint is medium grey. [Public Archives of Canada]

torpedoed ship behind her and she wheeled back for the convoy. Another U-boat appeared between her and the convoy, but disappeared into the convoy columns before action could be taken. As she joined her station, another ship exploded, revealing her attacker by her flames, and *Sackville* pursued. The U-boat dived, but *Sackville* laid a shallow pattern of depth charges around her a few moments later. The U-boat's bows broached the surface, followed by sixty feet of her hull casing. She rose perpendicular in the air and then, after hanging there awesomely for a few moments, she slid under, still at the same angle, belching air in huge bubbles. *Sackville*, to insure her kill, placed a further ten charges in the still-boiling waters, and a huge oil slick burst to the surface, followed by an underwater explosion that was felt throughout the hull. Add a "probable kill" to *Sackville*'s score.

An hour later *Sackville* sighted another U-boat, just 125 yards on her port side, but lost it in the lowering fog. Half an hour later, the same U-boat crossed her bows at 200 yards, out of a dense patch of fog. *Sackville* went to full ahead to attempt to ram, but the U-boat turned bows-on and within moments was under the maximum depression of *Sackville*'s 4-inch. The U-boat and corvette raced past each other in opposite directions, *Sackville* turning on her beam ends and pursued. Thus began a mad zigzagging chase, with *Sackville* attempting to ram, the U-boat evading. However, the U-boat finally made a mistake in allowing herself to drift back from under the corvette's bows and the eager gunners put a 4-inch round into the base of the conning tower. Machine gun fire raked the bridge, killing some, but keeping others below and

OAKVILLE, in the fifth year of the war. Note the increased deterioration of the Western Approaches paint. At the waterline medium gray paint and rusty plate shows. Note the offset 271 radar. [Marcom]

away from the U-boat's armament. Suddenly the U-boat dived at full speed and an Asdic contact could not be obtained in the turbulant waters. Add a "probable damaged" to *Sackville*'s score.

The next kill occurred in the Caribbean on the night of 27 August. HMCS *Oakville*, one of the seven escorts for a tanker convoy numbering 29 ships. She was part of the Canadian escort force that had been assigned to this sector to assist the American escorts in gaining experience. The evening of the 27th was perfect U-boat weather with a full moon and a light ruffle on the surface. A U.S. patrol plane radioed the escorts that she had surprised a surfaced U-boat in the brilliant moonlight and partially disabled it with a depth charge. *Oakville* detached herself and sped to the spot, obtaining a good contact as she neared. Down rumbled the first patterns, and with the explosions the damaged U-boat wallowed to the surface. *Oakville* attempted to ram, but she oversteered and missed, with *U-94* bumping and scraping down the corvette's port side. The crew hammered away with everything that could be depressed that far, with the 20 mm Oerlikons clearing the U-boat's decks of gun crew and smashing the deck gun itself. *Oakville* attempted to

Lieutenant Commander A. Easton, RCNR, receives the Distinguished Service Cross from Admiral L. Murray, 21 February 1944. Easton, at this time, was commander of the destroyer SASKATCHEWAN. Note the entwined Reserve rings on Easton's uniform. He had been commander of BADDECK, mentioned earlier. [Public Archives of Canada]

BATTLEFORD, as she appeared in 1941. Note she still has her mainmast, sweeper gear, and two machine guns in the bandstand, but does have the horrible SW2CQ radar antenna. Overall medium gray. [Marcom]

LUNENBERG, seen here in a 1943 Light Admiralty Disruptive pattern, using off-white and dark gray. Note the star rocket rails are loaded. The 252 IFF for 271 at cross-trees. Wash on rails caused a row with shore authorities who questioned why it was there. The answer read: "Submit: To dry." [Marcom]

ram again, but missed, as the U-boat sheared away with what little steerage way was left. Nothing could be depressed far enough and the frustrated gunners hurled pop bottles and anything else handy at the U-boat's bridge. As the corvette's stern surged past the officer in charge dropped two depth charges set at their minimum setting, which promptly blew up after only a few moments in the water, further disabling the U-boat, and rattling the fillings in the deck crews' mouths on the corvette. The German crew began to surge out of the hatches, as *Oakville* came alongside.

Sub-Lieutenant Harold Lawrence and Petty Officer A. J. Powell headed the boarding party and they found the conning tower riddled with 20 mm holes and the mutilated bodies of the crew scattered about. They ordered two survivors below, but were forced to shoot both as they tried to attack the party with large wrenches. Lawrence shouted down the hatch to surrender in his best German (it was his *only* German!), but received no reply. However, a few moments later twenty crew members came up through the hatch, after obviously scuttling the submarine. Scrambling below, Lawrence found the deck plates awash, which was enough to send him back on deck. He ordered the Germans over the side, and then followed suit to be picked up by the corvette as the U-boat settled beneath the waves quietly.

December 1942 saw Convoy ON-154 westbound, entering the "Black Pit" just before

LOUISBURG II. This photo shows a beautiful Admiralty Disruptive pattern of 1943, hence this has to be the second by this name. Colors are off-white/medium-dark green. [Public Archives of Canada]

VILLE DE QUEBEC, as she appeared in 1944. Unusual point is the 20 mm mounted in the bandstand; also four more forward of the bandstand. A total of seven Oerlikons are on this ship. Note she is assigned to an English escort group, the 62nd. Paint is a modified Western Approaches in three tones: light green, off-white, and light blue. [Author's collection]

Christmas Day. The Candian destroyer *St. Laurent*, with five corvettes (*Napanee, Battleford, Shediac, Kenogami,* and *Chilliwack*) were escorting 44 merchant ships, a special service ship (or CAM — Catapult Armed Merchantman — ship) *Fidelity*, and a rescue ship, a fairly new feature. A furious gale brewed up, but not before a shadowing U-boat had collected 6-8 members of the pack to the convoy.

The gale intervened before the U-boats could attack, scattering and damaging the ships, as the frantic escorts attempted to keep the convoy together.

On the 27th, at 0200 hours, two ships were torpedoed; by the end of the next two hours, two more. The U-boats broke off at dawn, but the gale continued unabated. The escorts began to run short on fuel with the extra steaming they had done. As darkness fell on the 28th, *Chilliwack* was forced to try the new procedure of refuelling at sea, with the tender *Scottish Heather*, but only a few gallons had flowed when the tanker itself was torpedoed and with it any hopes of fuel that the escorts may have had.

The U-boat pack continued to gather and the escorts' fuel situation became worse. The CAM ship *Fidelity* attempted to launch her caterpult aircraft to force the U-boats under, but it collided with a wave and sank, leaving the crew bobbing in the wash.

That night, the 29th, the U-boats attacked, with *Battleford* making the first radar contact, which she illuminated with starshell. The harsh light showed *four* U-boats steering straight for the convoy in a line-astern formation. *Battleford* opened fire and the U-boats made an ordered retreat, drawing the corvette after them.

Meanwhile, the remaining U-boats attacked from all directions at the same time. *Kenogami* reported a contact and then *Napanese* sighted another conning tower. The U-boats bore into the convoy, firing salvoes at point-blank range from all tubes. The merchantmen fired their tracer machine guns to show the escorts where the U-boats were. Snowflake indicated the torpedoed vessels. Within two hours, nine ships had gone down. The U-boats withdrew at dawn to replenish torpedo tubes and to rest their crews.

The fuel situation was rapidly reaching the crisis point with most escorts. *Battleford* and *Shediac* had to leave for the Azores because of the low fuel situation. *Battleford* actually towed *Shediac* into harbor!

With only four escorts left, the chances of defense were impossible. The senior officer ordered the ships of the convoy to scatter and make their own way as best they could. This obviously was an order of desperation and a sign of defeat. Even the abrupt breaking-off of U-boat contact was of no help. The convoy system had been broken by sheer numbers of U-boats. The prospects for 1943 appeared very grim, at least in the North Atlantic. To make matters worse, seventeen corvettes had been withdrawn for the Dieppe experiment, and then sent on to the Mediterranean for 'Operation Torch', the invasion of North Africa. Things indeed seemed black.

The request for corvettes for 'Operation Torch' had been a hard one to make, in view of the grim North Atlantic losses, but on 10 September 1942, the corvettes *Louisburg, Woodstock,* and *Prescott* had sailed from Halifax for the United Kingdom, where their armament was greatly increased. The other twelve corvettes committed to this scheme had additional guns installed at Halifax and sailed for England

VILLE DE QUEBEC, as she appeared on January 13, 1943 as part of 26 EG, Western Med. Fleet, during the attack that finally put U-224 on the bottom. Two-colour Admiralty Disruptive (1943 pattern) is not standard for the Mediterranean; some attempt has been made to paint over with medium gray (see bow back to 4-inch platform). [Ken MacPherson]

PORT ARTHUR, as she appeared in 1944. Note switch back to light gray. Also black silhouette pennant numbers. [Public Archives of Canada]

during October and November, earning their keep as escorts for eastward bound convoys. Only *Louisburg, Prescott, Woodstock, Weyburn, Lunenburg,* and the British corvette *Nasturtium* from the North Atlantic runs were prepared for the landings at Algiers, Oran, and Casablanca, as British shipyards had been swamped under with alterations to invasion vessels. The others, *Ville de Quebec, Port Arthur, Baddeck, Alberni, Summerside, Regina, Calgary, Kitchener, Camrose, Moose Jaw,* and *Algoma* followed them to the 'Med' for later operations. These corvettes were to escort convoys from the United Kingdom to Gibraltar and on to the base at Bone, in Tunisia, with intermediate supply stops at Oran, Arzeu, Algiers, Bougie, and Philippeville. The war was to prove very different in the Mediterranean.

WAR IN THE 'MED'

War in the 'Med' was as different as night and day. Here the U-boat hunted alone, not in packs, and aircraft attacks by Italian and German planes was much greater than in the North Atlantic, where it was only existent on the Murmansk/Archangel runs. Many mistakes were made by Canadian corvettes, which British units with three years' experience with the Italian/German navies and air forces, found amusing or irritating. Such was the case in December 1943 when a Canadian corvette, newly arrived, rammed a torpedo, thinking it a submarine. The British unit in charge congratulated her on her mistake with some very acid comments. However, the Canadians would learn.

The Canadian corvette, *Ville de Quebec*, collected the first trophy on 13 January 1943. She was a member of an escort group with a convoy, 90 miles off Algiers, when she obtained a good underwater contact. The first pattern of depth charges brought the U-boat's bows to the surface. The corvette's starboard Oerlikons engaged and a few moments later she rammed the U-boat forward of the conning tower. The U-boat tilted away from the corvette's bows, righted herself and then sank within five minutes. Under water explosions and flotsam marked her grave. The kill had taken ten minutes.

January 22nd saw the next kill in the 'Med'. Port Arthur and the British destroyer *Antelope* ended the short life of the Italian submarine *Tritone* (746 tons, built in 1942). She had sailed from Cagliari on 17 January 1943, and after faults had shown themselves in the diving gear, she was trundled off to Tunisia by the obstinate captain, over the chief engineer's protests, on 18 January. A few days later, she sighted a convoy and approached to within *500* yards at periscope depth, although the diving gear made diving difficult. The captain was about to commence attack, when the trim was lost and she plunged to 60 feet, out of control. After some 'fruity' remarks from the Italian engineer about vain-glorious captains, the submarine was finally gotten under control and brought back to periscope depth. Her trim was precarious at best and impossible to keep in an attack attitude long enough to launch torpedoes. The captain, frantic, forgot about asdic and radar and the great 'feather' that his periscope caused in his eagerness to press home his hopeless attack.

Port Arthur had detected her at 1,700 yards, and followed her echo to within 400 yards where her hydrophones had picked up *Tritone*'s propellers. The Italian captain, in one of his saner moments, spotted the corvette and promptly panicked and dove to avoid the escort. But, *Port Arthur*'s depth charges knocked out the main fuses, the electric motors were disabled, and pipes and tanks of the pressure system bent, cracked or distorted, as well as several fuel tanks which leaked a tell-tale slick to the surface. *Tritone* sank slowly till she grounded on her side in almost 400 feet of water. The crew used the last of the compressed air to check the plunge further and force herself to the surface, where she provided a surprise to *Port Arthur* who had lost her asdic in the first attack. *Antelope* had just joined her, when *Tritone* wallowed her way to the surface 700 yards off *Port Arthurs'* bows. The corvette and destroyer opened fire with everything they possessed, and *Port Arthur* attempted to ram, but had to shear off because of *Antelope*'s firing. The Italians attempted to man the guns and fire their torpedoes, but the crew took this chance to boil up through the hatches, where the first were killed by a direct hit by *Antelope*'s 4.7 inch. *Port Arthur* ceased fire to allow the crew to escape, as *Tritone* was settling fast. The rejoicing Italian survivors were picked up, glad to be out of the war. The reward? One thousand dollars from their namesake city, in appreciation of their first kill.

However many submarines and aircraft attacks in the 'Med', the Battle of the Atlantic had taken an upward turn for the U-boats. It was clear that the seventeen corvettes would have to return to the Atlantic. But a few actions were in store for the corvettes yet.

On 6 February, convoy KMS-8 from Gibraltar for Bone, Tunisia, was being escorted by nine Canadian and six British corvettes. About 36 miles from Oran, three German planes attacked the escorts from the low evening sun. Near misses were the only damage to one of the British corvettes, and *Louisburg* engaged a second aircraft diving at her masthead. The bomber released a torpedo which struck *Louisburg* midships and she began to settle rapidly. The 'abandon ship' was given and the men took to the life rafts and boats. The *Louisburg* sank in four minutes, with the loss of Lt. Cdr. W. F. Campbell, RCNVR, and 37 men and officers. Most of the losses were caused by exploding depth charges — a definite hazard in any escort sinking.

February 18, 1943 saw the corvette *Regina* avenge her sister ship. Near Philippeville, at about 2310 hours, a radar blip was reported to the bridge. *Regina* investigated and the radar contact became firmer. Suddenly the image disappeared from the screen; the U-boat had spotted her and crash-dived to avoid her. A pattern of depth charges were dropped and about ten minutes later, after all hope of contact had faded, the wake of the fleeing submarine was seen. She had been forced to the surface at some distance and was now making a run for it. *Regina* poured a murderous fire of 20 mm shells into the U-boat's bridge and deck spaces. The U-boat returned her fire, until *Regina*'s 4 inch entered the fray, hitting the base of the conning tower. The U-boat turned out to be an Italian submarine, as *Regina* closed on her, and the crew now filed onto the decks in surrender. After circling the disabled submarine to make sure there

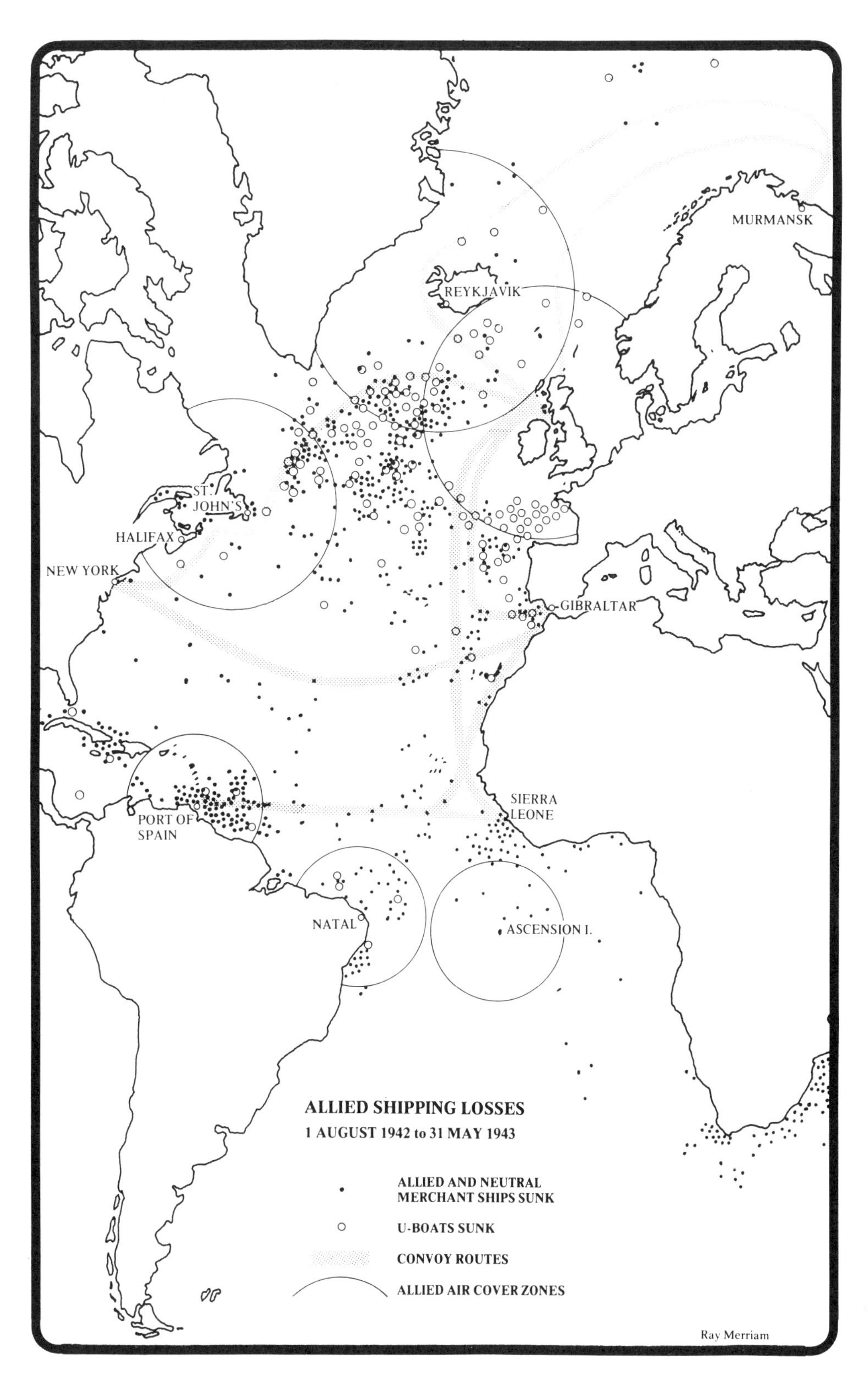

wasn't a second, *Regina* came alongside and embarked the prisoners. The Italian captain, first lieutenant, navigator, and sixteen ratings had been killed by the Oerlikons. She sank from the 4 inch damage about 10 minutes later.

On 22 February, the corvette *Weyburn*, dispatched from Gibraltar to escort a U.K.-bound convoy, struck a mine, just as she joined the convoy. The explosion occured on the port side, midships and tore a large hole, buckled the maindeck and split the funnel from top to bottom. She appeared stable in the aftermath, so the 'abandon ship' was not sounded and the deck crew scurried about securing the depth charge detonators, other than the last two which were jammed in the racks in such a way that the detonators could not be turned to 'safe'.

The British W Class destroyer *Wivern* came alongside and began to remove the wounded. Suddenly, 20 minutes later, *Weyburn* gave a shudder and her bows rose into the air and she

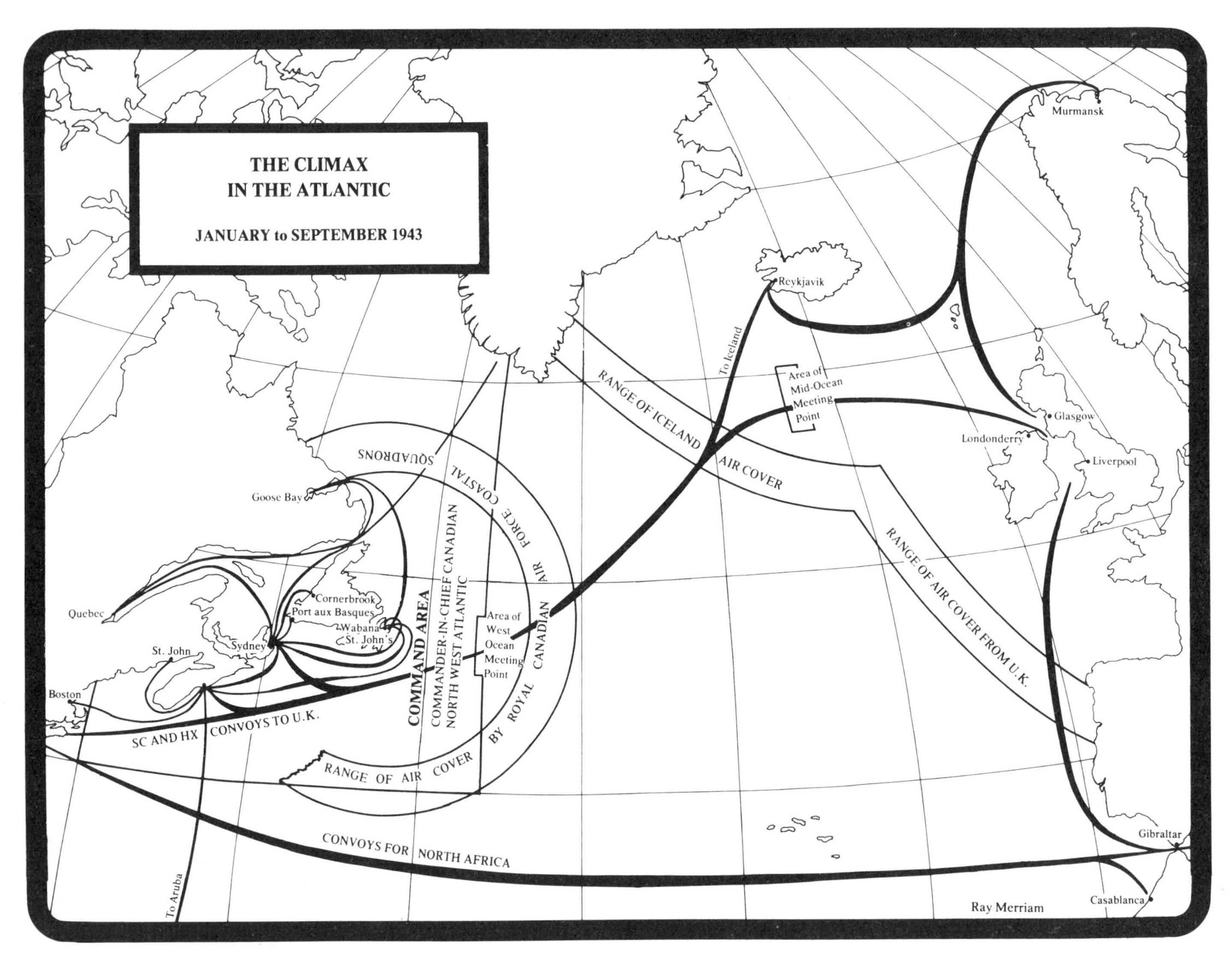

REGINA in 1942. Three-tone Western Approaches paint, with the medium gray showing through. Note the foremast is still ahead of the bridge, the compass platform has been widened to accomodate the two 20 mm Oerlikons, but the 271P radar has not been fitted. Corvettes as a rule did not make much smoke, hence we have a sloppy engineer on duty. [Public Archives of Canada]

began to settle rapidly by the stern, with *Wivern* still secured alongside. As the combined crews frenzily tried to cut the ropes securing the two vessels, the two depth charges, now underwater and armed, exploded. The captain, Lt. Cdr. T. M. Golby, and other senior officers on the bridge were killed, as well as survivors in the water and on deck.

Wivern was severely damaged with buckled decks and bulkheads, plus hull damage which disabled the propeller shafts. The mess decks were in chaos and the wardroom had to be used as the operating theater. The medical officer had had both ankles broken in the explosion, but directed the S.B.A. in operations and volunteers in first aid, despite his pain.

Lieutenant W. A. B. Garrard, of *Weyburn*, had both feet crushed, but insisted that the ratings be treated first. After all that could be done was done, then the M.O. directed the S.B.A. in how to amputate Garrad's feet, which was done without anesthetic, but Garrard never complained, much to the wonder of the hands present. His ordeal became a legend among those who knew him.

By March 1943 the Mediterranean was adjudged to be settled enough to release the Canadian corvettes, one by one, back to the United Kingdom. They were desperately needed in the North Atlantic, where the U-boat havoc was at an all-time high. Donitz had taken over from Raeder, who had resigned in protest to Hitler's decision to scrap the German capital ships. Admiral Donitz immediately switched all naval priorities over to U-boat production, in cooperation with Speer, and new U-boat types, as well as stepped-up crew training, produced an increase in U-boat activity in the fall of 1943 through the use of larger packs and more bold attacks.

However, 'old man winter' shoved both belligerants into survival positions. December 1942 through March 1943 saw the worst weather experienced in the North Atlantic in memory. This four month period only saw ten random days when a gale of some sort wasn't blowing. Damage to convoy ships was staggering, with sinkings from weather, not enemy action. Escort vessels fared no better; less than 70% of 231 escort vessels in the North Atlantic were operational at any time.

No calendar date would be accurate in describing the winter offensive of 1943. It had its beginnings in 1942, with more U-boats coming into service than were being sunk. January saw more than 100 U-boats in the Atlantic, mainly in the Western Sector. That month saw a wolf pack attack a tanker convoy in the Caribbean, sinking seven of the nine tankers composing it!

February's weather kept all combatants fighting for their lives, instead of each other, with its vicious gales and mountainous seas.

Any indication of the viciousness of the U-boat attacks, when the weather allowed could be seen in the records of Convoy ON-66 (westbound). Sixty-three vessels left Northern Ireland and amid numerous U-boat warnings, thirteen were forced to return to the United Kingdom with storm damage; one more, for the same reason, near Iceland; twelve more were torpedoed; nine turned up as stragglers, and only twenty-eight reached St. John's, Newfoundland, as a convoy. *Trillium*, a corvette, showed up with *160* survivors, plus her crew, aboard, with them sandwiched in every horizontal space, with no food, little water, and *very* little fuel (less than one ton!). She sailed within 48 hours with an eastbound convoy.

The Atlantic Convoy Conference of March 1943, changed the decision of the Atlantic Charter back in 1941, putting North Atlantic convoys as far east as Iceland (MOMP) under American control. This now reverted to the Canadians from New York, north and east to 40 degrees west, roughly a rectangle. This now came under Commander

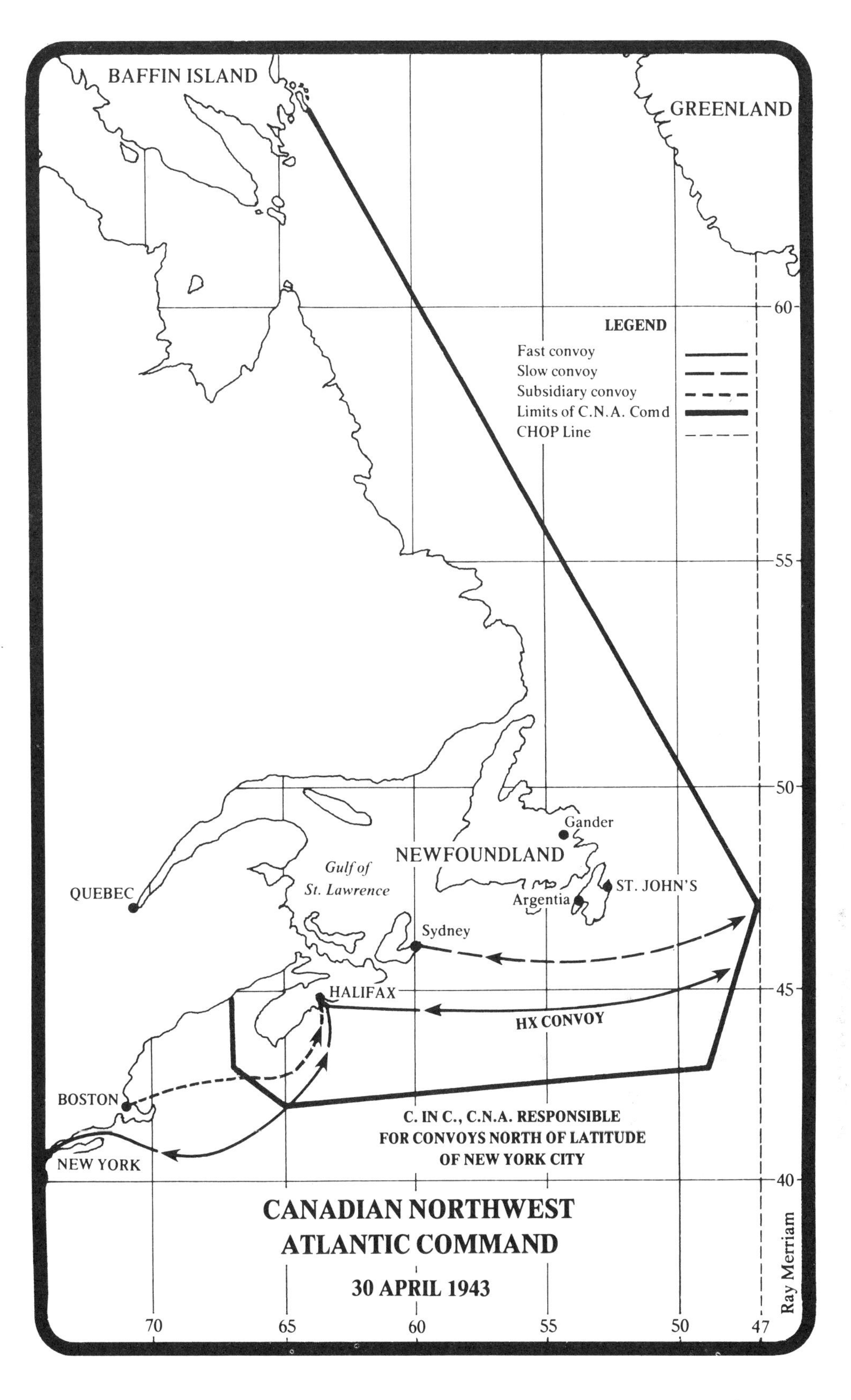

WEYBURN, 1943. Western Approaches three-tone, although shadow makes it seem there is light gray, there isn't; off-white. Canadian ships preferred the sharp edged pattern throughout the years of the war. Note the splinter mats, .303 machine guns on the bridge wings, 271 offset and hidden by the compass house. Also a SW2CQ yagi antenna up top. [Public Archives of Canada]

LA MALBAIE, 1943, about to come alongside to pass articles over. She has fallen into the wave trough behind the destroyer and collided with the following wave. Note her nose-down attitude, three-tone paint, 271 and SW2CQ radars. [R. A. Broomer, Author's collection]

A photo of an east-bound convoy from an escorting corvette. Note how low the ships' silhouettes appear. The depth charge thrower shows well in the right corner of the photo as well as the dan buoys and carley float. [Ken MacPherson]

HMCS BARRIE, in June 1943—heavy seas persisted all summer, but winter of 1943-1944 was to prove even worse. BARRIE is in two-tone medium green/off-white paint, has her mast aft, 271Q radar, bridge widened, and compass house is gone. Asdic hut now overhangs the bridge front. Note the white water and spray. [Public Archives of Canada]

in Chief, Canadian Northwest Atlantic, Rear Adm. L. W. Murray, with headquarters at Halifax. South of this line, the U. S. Navy took over control, and east of 40 degrees west, the Royal Navy. At the time of the decision, escort division was running 50% British, 48% Canadian, and 2% American in the North Atlantic, so this can be seen as a realistic assignment of responsibility.

Canada received back the seven corvettes that she had transferred to U. S. Navy control in the Caribbean, and the U.K. transferred six over-age Fleet destroyers, of which five were commissioned into the R.C.N. immediately. With the return of the seventeen corvettes 'loaned' to the British for the 'Med', the strain was relieved some on the existing escorts already in the North Atlantic, thus relieving the possibility of a collapse of the escort service. Also the expanded building program promised more ships in the near future. Canada entered this crucial year of the war in the North Atlantic with a very large responsibility indeed.

Convoy SC-121 was to prove the new strength of the U-boat arm. In the last days of February and the first ten days of March, twelve ships were lost. Escorts came and went, with fuel shortages and mechanical breakdowns or requests for assistance from other areas. Southwesterly and westerly gales battered the 51 ships of the convoy, destroying all semblance of order or organization.

U-boat sightings had started 6 March, when the convoy was to the southwest of Iceland. By nightfall estimates of ten U-

HMS RAJAH, as seen as in 1944, as an escort carrier built for the Royal Navy based on a merchant C3 hull design. Carriers of this type were largely responsible for closing the "Black Gap" in the North Atlantic and severely limiting U-boat cruising and daylight attacks."

boats were confirmed. By morning one ship was sunk, with only three survivors being picked up. The gale became fiercer and the convoy began to separate. Two more ships went down that night; five more the following, without one escort being able to make or hold a contact. The total losses for March were 627,000 tons; not the highest of the war, but they were ominous in that 75% of these losses occurred in convoy, under the best protection the Allies could provide.

Meanwhile, the first British support groups started in April and soon showed their worth. The Support Groups, comprised of destroyers, frigates, sloops, and *five* escort carriers of the Americans, would prove the U-boat's undoing; it would close the air gap over the central North Atlantic where the U-boat had preyed for so long without airborne interference. The Groups' only job was to relieve beleaguered convoys of their U-boat attackers — the first hunter-killer groups.

On 25 April, 300 miles off the tip of Greenland, a threatened convoy was relieved to see six friendly warships appear over the horizon — one of the Special Support Groups. It included the escort carrier *Biter* who launched her special anti-submarine aircraft, who soon located the wolf pack and made possible the kill of one of them by surface units. Thirty-five merchant ships were sunk that month, with only the loss of eight U-boats, *but* five were sunk by aircraft alone, and cooperation between plane and surface units netted another.

HMS BATTLER with fighter bombers aboard.
[Author's collection]

Convoy HX-237 which left New York on 1 May and arrived at the Mid-Ocean Meeting Point on the 5th, had had *Biter*'s Support Group along as distant escort but had not had any problems from U-boats at all, although sightings and attacks had occurred at various points around the convoy's position. The close escort had included the corvettes *Morden, Drumheller,* and *Chambly.* The long-range Liberators plus aircraft from *Biter* were aloft whenever the fog lifted and carried the attack to the U-boats, far removed from the convoy. The 12th proved a surprise for one U-boat: a Liberator bomber caught her on the surface and sank it — 1,200 miles from base! The 14th saw another U-boat sunk and five more pounded. The pack could no longer form.

The 15th would mark another nail in the U-boats' collective coffin. *Chambly* spotted a U-boat on that same day and gave chase. The U-boat, remaining on the surface soon began to pull away from her and leave her behind. But the U-boat knew nothing of the Support Group, elements of which lie dead ahead of her. A bomber attacked her, drove her under, marked the area with dye, steered *Chambly* and two British destroyers

DRUMHELLER as she appeared in 1944-1945. This type of paint pattern was widely used by the RCN in the last year of the war. The ship is off-white, with a medium or light gray false hull. Note the great length of stove pipe from the galley. [Author's collection]

The starboard side of the compass platform, with the rosette compass in the foreground. Signaller is using hand-held signal light, aldis type. Note escort carrier BITER in background, mixed with freighters. [Marcom]

to the sight where the U-boat was about to receive the benefits of a new anti-submarine weapon — Hedgehog. Sixteen seconds later, after the attack began, a huge explosion and oily flotsam marked the grave of the U-boat.

The idea behind Hedgehog was that asdic contact would not be lost, as in a standard depth charge attack. The charges were fired well ahead of the ship, while a firm contact was maintained, not when the contact was lost in the cone of silence below the sender head or in the noise of the ships' machinery and propellers.

May 16th saw another kill by Hedgehog, which was shared by the Canadian corvette *Drumheller.* HX-237 had lost a straggler to a torpedo and *Drumheller* picked up 15 survivors, when a Sunderland flying boat was observed about six miles away, circling low. Her Aldis lamp informed *Drumheller* that she was over a U-boat, which sent her racing for the spot. When she arrived it was to find the U-boat battling with the flying boat and one of *Biter*'s bombers. *Drumheller* opened fire and the U-boat dived. *Drumheller* depth charged her, and was joined by the British frigate *Lagan*, who was Hedgehog-equipped. The Canadian corvette directed *Lagan* to the asdic contact, who laid a neat pattern on the contact point. An explosion followed, and after a few moments an air bubble 60 feet in diameter and a liberal amount of debris littered the area. Another kill for Hedgehog. But Hedgehog would never really replace the 300 pound depth charge.

Sinkings that month were 157,000 tons versus 37 U-boats sunk and 32 damaged. At last U-boat losses were more than new ones coming into service!

September 12th saw ONS-18 leave the United Kingdom for the western journey. On 15 September ON-202 followed it, with the escort group consisting of the Canadian destroyer *Gatineau,* corvettes *Drumheller* and *Kamloops,* plus the British destroyer *Icarus* and the corvette *Polyanthus.* ON-202, being the faster convoy overtook ONS-18 by the 19th, when U-boat transmissions were intercepted and decoded in London. The U-boat "vacation" of the summer months was over, the escorts were informed by late afternoon. The convoys joined and the new Support Group — consisting of the Canadian ships *St. Croix, St. Francis, Chambly, Sackville,* and *Morden,* with the British frigate *Itchen* — was ordered to join the combined escort screen. The actual union of convoys occurred on the 20th at dusk in a gathering fog. By dark 63 merchant ships were still out of station. The Support Group formed the outer screen, while the close Support Escort, which included a merchant aircraft carrier, formed as best they could to protect the convoy. The only actions to occur that night was the British frigate who under mysterious circumstances lost 30 feet of her stern to a suspected U-boat, and the loss of *St. Croix* to torpedoes, leaving 81 survivors. Also, later, the loss of *Polyanthus*, with only one survivor. All had been hit from astern. These were the first attacks by Germany's new secret weapon, the acoustic torpedo, which came as a complete surprise to the Allies.

Nine attacks occurred on the 21st. Losses were one U-boat rammed and sunk; two more damaged. The night of the 22nd saw attacks begin at 2130 hours. *Morden* illuminated a U-boat ahead of the convoy,

Another shot of BARRIE in June 1943, showing her breasting a swell. Note how the short hull is out of sync with the wave, the bow is clear, yet the rudder and propeller are coming clear at the same time. Note the 252 IFF appears to be on top of the 271 radar. The 291 air warning can be seen as well at mast-top. [Marcom]

DRUMHELLER, taken in late 1944-1945. Note how the paint has been worn away at the waterline. Overall off-white, light gray or blue false hull. [Public Archives of Canada]

HMCS ST. FRANCIS, shown here in 1941, has a little of everything for everyone. The 286M 'bedstead' antenna is very prominent, as is the mixture of camouflage patterns. Off-white, light gray, light green and blue, plus dark blue to alter the bow silhouette. As can be seen there is very little sheer or rake on these former U.S. Navy World War I destroyers, making them a miserable sea boat for the North Atlantic. But they did the job. [Marcom]

SACKVILLE as she appeared in the winter of 1943-1944. Note the SW2 antenna still fitted although the 271 is now mounted. She appears to be overall medium gray, but the rust streaks and general weathering make it difficult to tell. Note damage to the bow, doubtless from a chance encounter with a wharf. [Marcom]

MORDEN, in 1946, in what appears to be Shelburne, Nova Scotia. Note the extended bridge, yet the compass house is still retained. Light gray overall, with the usual weathering at the waterline midships. [Marcom]

which was shelled by several escorts. *Itchen* illuminated another with her searchlight, but disappeared in a huge explosion, another victim of an acoustic torpedo.

By the 23rd, when shore-based aircraft brought relief, four escorts and seven merchant ships were sunk.

Within seventeen days all escort vessels were being equipped with "Foxer" devices, later replaced by 'CAT' (Canadian Anti-Torpedo) gear. These devices made such a racket that they deceived and rendered ineffective the vaunted "Zaunkonig" torpedo. CAT consisted of two pieces of special pipe that when towed astern could alternatively be made to chatter or be quiet. It worked, and to this day CAT, in improved forms, are still carried.

With the surrender of Italy, further British escort vessels were released to the North Atlantic, making the attack role of the U-boat more difficult and dangerous.

The Canadian Navy by the end of 1943 consisted of 306 operational warships, 71,549 men manning them, and 4,453 women in shore installations.

The work for the Canadian corvettes

HMCS CAMROSE, November 1943. Note the very neat Western Approaches three-tone paint in light green/light blue/off-white. Note the Mark II gear still on the stern of both corvettes. Also, she has the final bridge configuration and extra 20 mm armament. [Royal Canadian Navy via Author's collection]

remained convoy escort at the end of 1943 and, in fact, RCN ships had largely taken over escort duties from North America to Great Britain, releasing British units for the forthcoming effort in Europe.

The work was fairly routine to those accustomed to the hectic pace of 1942-1943, but could be just as deadly. Ships were still lost in the winter of 1943-1944 and men still drowned. The convoys had grown to enormous sizes and had become unwieldy to say the least. A prime example was related to me by the commander of HMCS *Royalmount* that occurred in January 1944 with an east-bound convoy:

> "I don't remember how many ships we had to convoy but, of course, being west bound they were all light — and most of them could float on a heavy dew and every bloody time it came on to blow these bloody merchantmen would get blown all over the Western Ocean — and it would take us days, literally, to gather them up — just like a sheep dog and hundreds of sheep running all over the lot. This crossing, and now you can believe this or not, but it took us twenty-one days — and we averaged 4.2 knots for the whole voyage and we did 3.6 knots for seven days. I'll bet that you can walk 3.6 knots along any sidewalk! Try it!"

Or this passage by the same chap, just prior to June 1944:

> "Speaking of convoys, I remember so vividly being called to Adm. Taylor's office one afternoon, in St. John's, and being told of the convoy that we would be escorting when we sailed in the morning. It was just prior to D-Day when just about everything that was movable was being transported to Europe. We sailed the following morning and as soon as we had cleared the gap I mustered the troops aft and told them what a tremendous experience we were to have — as on the following day when we rendezvoused at WOMP (Western Ocean Meeting Place) where we were to join with the largest convoy that had ever been assembled — and Dear Dying Mabel — you should have seen the size of this thing coming over the horizon! It was a convoy of 158 ships and was disposed in twenty-one columns at half a mile apart — or ten and a half miles wide!"

Lieutenant James B. Lamb, RCNVR, taken in June 1943. He had just assumed command of HMCS MINAS, a minesweeper, but was from corvettes and would command CAMROSE in the Channel and Western Approaches of Britain until wars' end. Average age of captains: 26-27. Crew members: 22, in 1943. [Public Archives of Canada]

In each of the months of January through April, Canadian ships sank or helped sink one U-boat. In one week of March they had a large share in the destruction of three. And in May a Canadian warship was lost by sub action with heavy loss of life.

However, back to the chase. . . The Canadian corvette *Camrose* shared credit with the RN frigate *Bayntun* for the January kill in which heavy depth charge attacks sent a U-boat to the bottom with little evidence, other than a vast pool of oil, some flotsam, and a uniform cap.

The most striking example of the changing

Hepatica, as seen in June, 1944, while part of W-5, Western Local Escort Force, based in Halifax, N.S. This ship typifies the corvette in the last stages of the war, with Hedgehog, final bridge configuration. However, the pom-pom platform shows she is a 1939-40 Flower. Paint would appear to be overall G45, light grey. [Marcom]

CHILLIWACK, taken in 1941, she is another west coast-built corvette. The extra plate covers the trunk of the 4-inch magazine, as well as covering an area of crews' quarters. Overlapping, riveted plates show well. The galley stack shows its location well, instead of aft, and the mainmast is fitted. [Author's collection]

tactics evolving in the Battle of the Atlantic occurred in March. This marathon hunt — one of the longest of the war for Canadian naval units — occupied 32 hours from first contact to kill. Seven ships, five Canadian, two British, were involved in this hunt to exhaustion. Two hundred ninety-one depth charges carrying a total of 87,300 pounds of high explosives were required to bring the wiley U-boat to the surface. Fifteen hundred signals passed between the ships, during the rough weather hunt.

The Canadian destroyer *Gatineau* made the first contact at about 10:00 hours on the morning of 10 March. The contact wasn't particularly good and the destroyer was suffering from distiller defects, but she decided to play along and see what she had. She informed the senior ship, *St. Catherines*, that she had a contact, and laid her first pattern, which the U-boat promptly dodged. *St. Catherines* and the corvettes *Chilliwack* and *Fennel* joined the chase, and *Chaudiere*, another destroyer, and two corvettes circled the area, these vessels began to take turns depth charging the U-boat, first randomly, then through creeping attacks, where one vessel directs the other in the attack. None were successful.

The British destroyer joined in, relieving *Gatineau*, whose defects now compelled her to proceed to Londonderry. Admiralty informed the escorts that U-boat transmissions had been monitored, vectoring on the convoy, so *Icarus* and *Chaudiere* returned to the convoy, and detached from a support group the British frigate *Kenilworth Castle*, which took their place.

The attacks went on all night, with the contact being lost numerous times, as the U-boat twisted and turned at her maximum depths. The escorts decided to play tough and took up station keeping over the contact, with running lights burning so they could hold position. They were determined to wait him out, until either his batteries gave up or his air. 'CAT' gear was towed, on the chance the U-boat might launch a 'Gnat' acoustic torpedo, and when it was thought one might have been, a single depth charge was dropped, trying to fool the U-boat into thinking that she had hit one of the escorts.

About 05:00 hours, *Icarus* and *Chaudiere* rejoined, after escorting the convoy out of danger and the active attacks began again. *Kenilworth Castle* detached herself to rejoin the convoy, as she had knocked out her Asdic with a depth charge pattern. At 08:00 hours the active attacks resumed. About noon the U-boat escaped contact for over a half-hour, but contact was regained. A change of tactics was now necessary it was felt, to prevent the U-boat from escaping that night. Accordingly, no depth charges were to be dropped until 16:00 hours, and these confined to occasional, single drops to foil acoustic torpedoes.

The strategy worked; at 15:30 hours the U-boat surged to the surface off *Chilliwack*'s bows, low on power and air. A signalman on the bridge of the corvette opened fire immediately, hitting the conning tower repeatedly. Seconds later, the 4-inch and two pounder swung into action. As well, every hand that could lay hands on a Bren gun or rifle was blazing away. *Fennel* joined the turkey-shoot moments later and the crew began to emerge from the hatches, only to be blown away by fire, as the captain was. The German crew, seeing their captain dead, began to slide over the saddle tanks and into the water.

Chilliwack, intending to ram, came charging at the hulk, but upon seeing little in the way of return fire and the crew abandoning ship, veered off and with *St. Catherines* came as close as possible and lowered boarding parties in boats. *Chilliwack*'s boarding party won the race and boarded first. Signalman J.R. Starr, who had pasted the U-boat with 20 mm shells, climbed to the periscope shears and tied on a White Ensign, which brought cheers from both ships. The boarding party, as they slipped below, found chlorine gas, broken glass, and water in the hull. They did recover the Enigma code books, signal books, and anything else that looked interesting. Noticing the terror of the German guide, they deduced that demolition charges had probably been set and scrambled to the upper deck with their precious hoard.

The whaler from *St. Catharines* arrived just as they emerged, but a rogue wave suddenly upset both it and the boat from *Chilliwack*, leaving the crews swimming about in the water. *Fennel* and *Chaudiere* came in as close as possible and spent an hour picking up survivors from the water and the marooned Canadians on the U-boat's deck. The U-boat was still afloat, but towing in the pitching seas was clearly impossible, so *Icarus* sank her with a well-placed torpedo about 18:30 hours on the 6th.

CHILLIWACK's prize—U-744, March 1944. Note the 4-inch and 20 mm damage to the bridge. The White Ensign can be seen wrapped around what is left of the periscope shears. [Marcom]

WOODSTOCK in 1943, showing her three-tone paint to good advantage. Note her gunshield art of Donald Duck swatting a U-boat with his sailor hat. [Author's collection]

The stage was being set in early 1944 for "Operation Neptune" which was to secure the waters of the English Channel and shores of Normandy for the invasion. By mid-April, most corvettes had been withdrawn from the North Atlantic for refit, and forwarded to the United Kingdom for this operation. Nineteen[2] Canadian corvettes were slated for the invasion duties to occur off Normandy's shores. The commanding officers and navigation officers were sent to the Western Approaches Tactical Unit in Liverpool for retraining, and the crews were subjected to intensive training periods. They were to be ready by April for the

2. *Woodstock, Regina, Prescott, Camrose, Lunenburg, Baddeck, Rimouski, Trentonian, Mayflower, Drumheller, Louisburg II, Alberni, Mimico, Calgary, Summerside, Kitchener, Port Arthur, Moose Jaw,* and *Lindsay* were the nineteen corvettes that took part in Operation Neptune.

MAYFLOWER, as she appeared in 1943 after her refit. Note the main armament is trained at the camera. Paint is a 1942 Modified Light Admiralty Disruptive, using a off-white/medium gray combination. She has her 271 offset to starboard. [Public Archives of Canada]

Another shot of Louisburg II in 1943, showing a light grey/dark grey Admiralty Disruptive pattern paint scheme and her antenna/radar to good advantage. [Marcom]

invasion, which was supposedly fixed for summer.

Suddenly the long-awaited tasks were assigned; they were to move to their pre-invasion points!

Previously to this great occasion, most had been based in Liverpool and other southern ports and had been used to convoy Channel vessels. Now this experience in the Channel would pay off.

Woodstock and *Regina* were the first Canadian corvettes to commence the preliminary escort work for "Neptune". April 28th saw *Woodstock* escort tugs and tows to the Thames ports. *Regina* followed suit on the 29th. *Prescott, Camrose, Lunenburg, Baddeck,* and *Rimouski* soon followed with the wildly varied mixture of ships and barges to the assembly ports of southern England.

By 15 May, twelve of the nineteen corvettes had been re-equipped, trained, and engaged in the pre-invasion work. This was to be the corvette's job, to shelter the coastal convoys from the alarmed German surface units, from which the purpose of the convoys could not be hidden. This remained so up until the invasion date neared.

At 09:00 hours, on the morning of 31 May, five Canadian corvettes set the first wheels of the invasion in motion. *Trentonian, Mayflower, Drumheller, Rimouski,* and *Louisburg II,* with the British corvette *Nasturtium*, sailed from Oban, Scotland, escorting the convoy of tows and blockships which were intended for the artificial harbors of Normandy. They were slow and had a long distance to go; they would be passed by faster, more numerous ships into the Normandy approaches, but they were the first to leave.

June 5th. . .Portsmouth, Southampton, and the Solent were now empty. . .the invasion forces were committed. . . The nineteen Canadian corvettes were among the multitude of escorts moving beside their convoys, or waiting anxiously for their sailing hour. For most, the first convoys would consist of blockships, concrete barges, towed breakwaters, and pontoon sections for the artifical harbors, which were scheduled to arrive after the assault was well underway. *Trentonian, Mayflower, Drumheller, Rimouski,* and *Louisburg II* were standing by the blockships they had shepherded all the way from Scotland. *Alberni, Mimico, Lunenburg, Camrose, Baddeck, Prescott,* and *Calgary* were on short notice to sail with other tows and attendant tugs for the artificial harbors. *Regina, Summerside,* and *Woodstock* were already sailing along the south coast

HMCS SACKVILLE, one of the 1939-40 Original Flower Class corvettes ordered for the Royal Canadian Navy. She was built at St. John Shipyard, St. John, New Brunswick, as hull number 11 and commissioned into that service on 30 December 1941. SACKVILLE was engaged in the Eastern Escort Forces from day one, engaging two U-boats on the night of 3 August 1942. While engaged in covering a fellow escort attempting to tow a damaged merchantman, SACKVILLE engaged a 1,000 ton 'milch cow' U-boat, which was subsequently sunk by depth charges. Later that same date, a 700 ton U-boat was engaged in a surface action, with one 4 inch hit before the U-boat submerged and was lost.

In early 1945, SACKVILLE was taken out of active service and converted to a controlled loop layer, to assist with the acoustic minefield outside of Halifax Harbor. However, the war ended before she was completed. She served as a research vessel with the RCN until 1964, when she was loaned to the Bedford Institute of Oceanography, where she works to this day, although she is still a Naval Auxiliary.

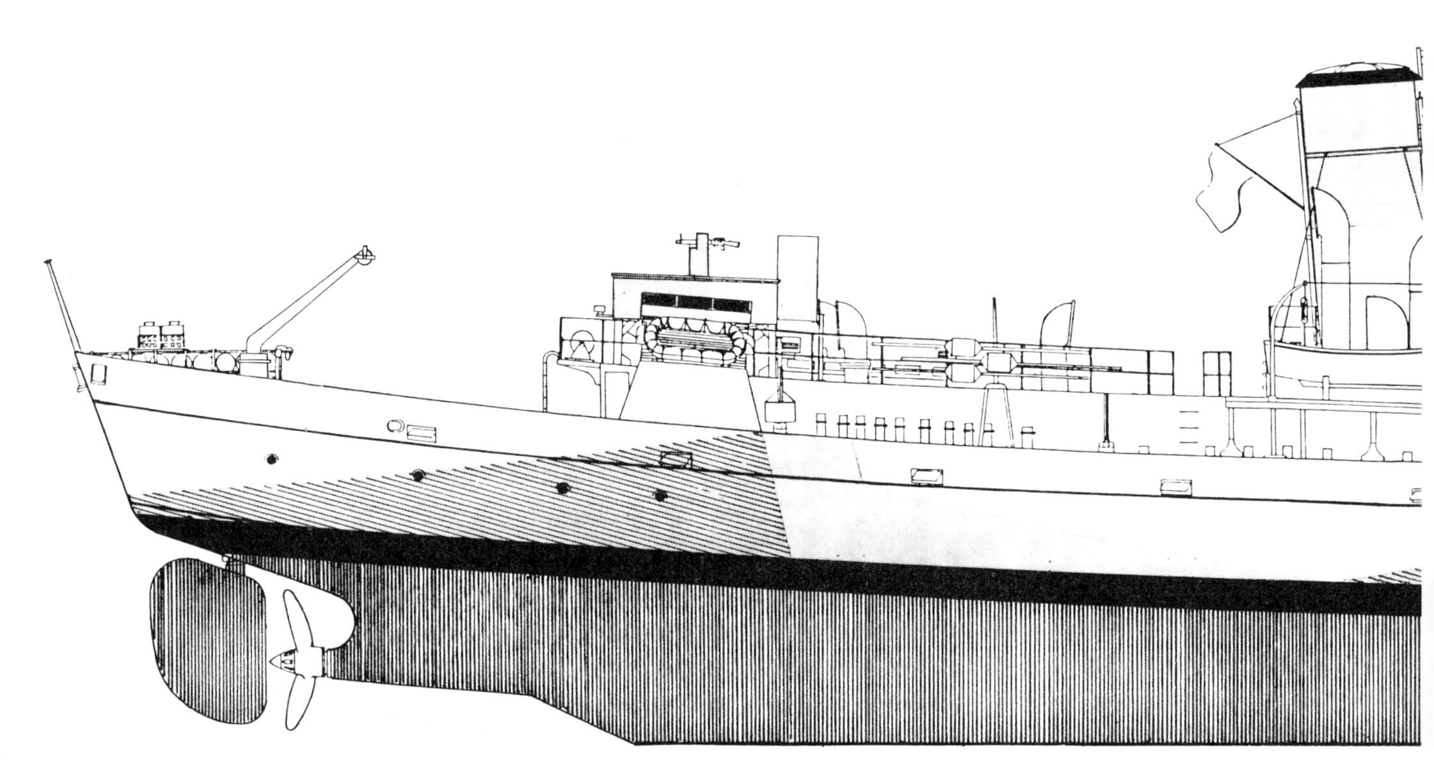

As depicted here, SACKVILLE sports a Western Approaches paint scheme, with color modifications. In 1942, when this scheme was present, substitutions were common as paint was scarce, especially in the newer shades. Here, the base color is Western Approaches off-white, with Western Approaches light green shadow panels. However, Deck Green has been used in place of the Western Approaches Blue. The underside of the barrel is painted pure white to dispell shadows and the minesweeping davits would be trained inboard to confuse viewing U-boats. Carley floats were keyed to the overall scheme. However, for realism, the sides would be scuffed and rust-streaked, showing the rigors of North Atlantic use.

NOTE:
Usually the bridge rails were covered by canvas dodgers and splinter matts, but these have been left off for detail's sake in this drawing. See photos for examples.

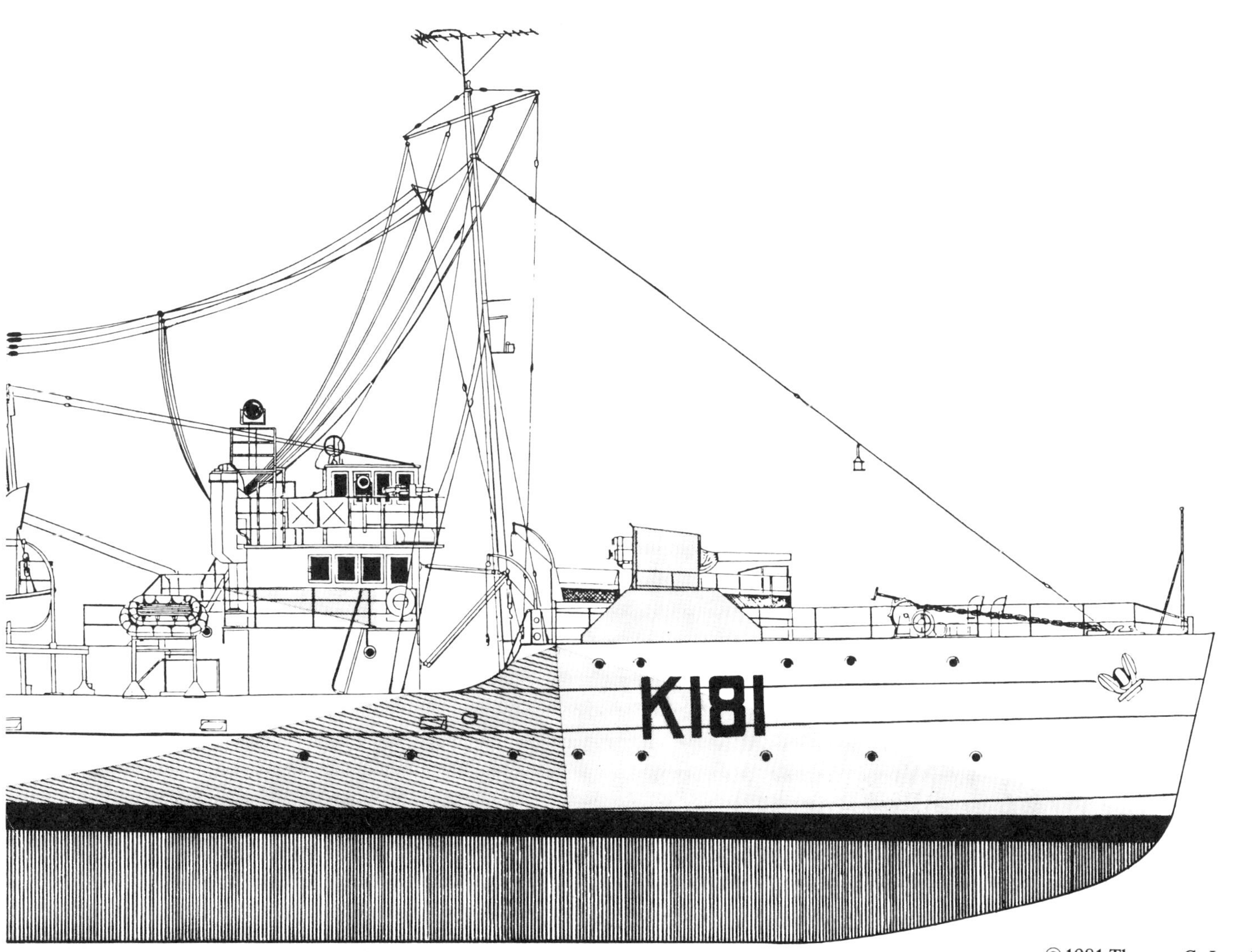

MIMICO, shown here in 1944, with 241 IFF aerial atop the 271, off-white overall, with light blue false bow wave. Note how the gun platform has been extended to provide for the hedgehog. [Marcom]

OWEN SOUND—a wartime release photo, the 271 radar has been blanked out as well as the DF loop, for some reason. Could be that the IFF was mounted here. Note the tubular framework on the bridge which had a canvas sun screen for protection of bridge personnel. Paint is off-white/light blue. [Marcom]

with twenty-seven Liberty ships, and *Kitchener* would leave Plymouth within the hour with a convoy of landing craft. *Port Arthur* and *Moose Jaw* had four fretful hours to wait before they could sail from Milford Haven, with a covy of fourteen transport ships. *Lindsay* would be the last, eleven hours behind them with nine merchantmen.

By early afternoon of the 6th, the following-up convoys began to arrive off the beaches. At 16:00 hours *Kitchener* arrived with her party of landing craft. By 04:20 hours on the 7th, *Alberni* and *Mimico* arrived with barges. *Trentonian, Mayflower,* and *Drumheller* eased their convoy of blockships between the narrow cleared passages a little before 12:00 hours. *Regina, Summerside,* and *Woodstock* had already arrived with their convoy of Liberty ships. *Prescott* arrived by 17:00 hours. Dawn of the 8th brought *Port Arthur, Moose Jaw, Camrose,* and *Baddeck. Rimouski, Louisburg,* and *Lunenburg* came about 05:30 hours. *Lindsay* arrived in the A.M. of the 9th, after a spirited engagement with E-boats while crossing. Poor *Calgary* was the last to see the beaches, as she had been shuttling convoys across the Channel and handing them off to other escorts on the Normandy side. She arrived on the 10th.

Here the corvettes would remain, escorting countless convoys across the Channel. The second day saw the artificial harbors secure and the corvettes returned to England to pick up pre-loaded merchantmen, which they escorted back to Normandy. During June, each of the Canadian corvettes made at least six trips to the beaches, and several made many more. They came under attack from E-boats on one or two

HMCS LA MALBAIE, again in 1943. The paint has been changed to light grey over off-white. The SW2 antenna is very prominent, as well as the extended platform that the 271 sits on. Note also that the foremast is still in front of the bridge at this late date. It was a tremendous hinderance to forward vision. [Marcom]

COLLINGWOOD, also in 1943, still has her short fo'c's'le and mast before the bridge, although the 271 and SW2 radars are evident. Three-tone Western Approaches paint. Also, the bridge has been extended to the sides. [Marcom]

occasions, and air attacks were far more common as well as the danger of mines, passive or adrift. On the whole, though it was pretty boring work, after the build-up they had received of how they should expect 50% losses to coastal batteries and aircraft.

They were on short notice even when they did hit port. In most cases the crews had only two four-hour periods of leave between 10 May and 22 June. *Camrose,* hardest hit, was unable to grant leave at all for over forty days. They must remain on call for whenever there was need for an escort. When they finally got leave it did them little good, as the ports were six-deep in other ships and the shore facilities were flooded. Besides, who had enough energy to go ashore? Most leave time was spent in sleep, doing your 'dhobey' (laundry), and mending clothes.

Each crossing was nerve-wracking, with having to navigate through narrow, cleared passages in minefields with ungainly merchantmen. As well, the many Asdic contacts were mostly sunken wrecks from other actions, but no one could take the chance, so depth charge it anyway. But there was *some* action. *Kitchener* and *Port Arthur* had one trip livened up by being near-missed by glider bombs. *Camrose, Baddeck,* and *Louisburg* fought off a series of attacks by E-boats on the night of 13 June. But the most harrowing of these experiences was on the 13th, in the early morning, when *Trentonian* was escorting the British cable-laying ship, *St. Margaret*. Jim Lamb, a friend of the *Trentonian*'s skipper wrote:

"In the hectic days following the first landings, on the Normandy beaches, the British cable ship *St. Margaret*, escorted by the Canadian corvette *Trentonian*, was laying a communication cable to the beachhead when they were attacked by an American destroyer. The attack, of course, was inexcusable; the American commanding officer had failed to read the signal informing him that the cable ship would be at work in his patrol area. But it was his persistence in the attack, once the identity of the cable ship was clear, that was positively criminal. The destroyer lit up the civilian ship with star shell, then pounded the unarmed vessel with salvoes from close range, shifting fire to the Canadian corvette when she tried to intervene. Eventually American bridge officers prevailed on their captain (a glory-hunter, they later explained to us) to cease fire. The American vessel then attempted to come alongside its shattered victim, but the fury of the British seamen, and of the Canadian corvette crew, prompted its chestfallen captain to make a prudent exit into the blackness of the night. The cable ship was a shell-torn wreck, littered with badly wounded

VILLE DE QUEBEC, 1944, in a 1943 Western Approaches paint scheme. A 20mm has been mounted in the bandstand, as well as four on deckhouse roof. Two-color scheme appears to be off-white with medium grey. [Author's collection]

men; her captain died in the arms of Bill Harrison, *Trentonian*'s commanding officer. The shattered ships — *Trentonian* had a hole through her engine room — limped back to Portsmouth." [From *Corvette Navy* by J. Lamb, by permission of the author.]

A tragic incident, but one that has occurred in many wars and places.

July and August passed fairly quietly for the corvettes and their never-ending convoys. Losses occurred regularly, whether to mines, E-boats, U-boats, or the occasional German aircraft. The odd U-boat still chanced slipping up the French coast to take a try at the bounteous shipping in the Channel.

One such vessel lost was *Regina*. On the evening of 8 August, while escorting a convoy off Trevose Head, Cornwall, one of the merchantmen was torpedoed. *Regina* came alongside immediately, and the Master reported that he had been mined. She appeared to be salvageable, and *Regina* ordered an American tank landing craft to take off the crew and rig a towline, while she stood guard. *Regina* backed off to about 100 yards as the tow was prepared to supervise.

Just as the towline became taut between the tank carrier and the merchantman, *Regina* blew up with a tremendous roar and sank in seconds. *Regina* had been the U-boat's second victim. Sixty-six survivors were rescued, ten seriously injured, and all suffering from shock. The remaining men had disappeared in the towering explosion, which had sent smoke and debris 100 feet into the air.

Many of *Regina*'s men would owe their lives to the American tank carrier, as crew members dove over the side to rescue half-drowned Canadian sailors. The corvette's Medical Officer, Surgeon-Lt. G.A. Gould, who although choking on oil and under morphia for other injuries, worked throughout the night to save lives in the American ships' wardroom.

Survivors of HMCS CLAYOQUOT alongside HMCS FENNEL, after being torpedoed off Halifax, Nova Scotia, 24 December 1944. Note the oily condition of the men, as well how exhausted they look, even though they have only been in the water for less than ten minutes. The oil, and the water's temperature killed in less time in the North Atlantic. [Marcom]

August brought some relief from the drudgery of the corvettes, and also changes in ships; *Port Arthur* and *Mayflower* were stationed alternatively as weather reporting ships in the open Atlantic, six hundred miles west of the Cornish coast. *Algoma* arrived in England to relieve *Woodstock*, which returned to Canada for a badly needed refit. *Ville de Quebec* and *Snowberry* arrived, and *Rimouski, Camrose, Prescott, Summerside,* and *Lunenburg* left for Canadian waters and re-assignment to convoy work. The remainder were assigned to anti-submarine patrols and *Alberni* was lost on one of these.

Alberni had distinguished herself on

PORT ARTHUR, in 1944, with very light gray paintwork. As can be seen, this is one of the Modified Flowers with sharper rake and flair to the bows. A full complement of radar aerials can be seen, as well as the extended position for the DF loop. Also the outline in black pennant numbers. [Marcom]

SNOWBERRY as she appeared on 25 November 1943. Note the position of her bandstand, marking her as one of the first Canadian corvettes to be built even though the fo'c's'le has been extended and bridge widened. Note the squarish 271P lantern house radar. The overall scheme is off-white with light blue panels and light green panels, which have suffered heavily from the weather and rust stains. Note also the uncovered hedgehog, abaft the 4-inch platform. [Public Archives of Canada]

26 July by shooting down a Ju 88 over the Neptune anchorage. Early on 21 August, she was ordered to relieve *Drumheller*, who was patrolling in an area off the Isle of Wight. At 11:46 hours, as she approached her station, she was hit by a torpedo and she was under the surface, other than her bows, in 20 seconds. As the ship sank, she twisted, drowning many of her crew in the water. The seas were choppy and there had been no time to release floats, so the situation looked grim. But within forty-five minutes, two British MTB's arrived and rescued three officers and 28 ratings. Fifty-nine men were lost.

The corvettes, with little time or opportunity for heroics, were the hardest hit of any Canadian naval force in Operation Neptune. Ninety men were killed and thirty wounded out of the total casualties of 120 killed and 159 wounded for Canada's naval committment.

November 1944 saw the next loss of a corvette, again in Canadian waters. On the 25th, the corvette *Shawinigan* was lost with *all* hands, while on an independent patrol in the Cabot Strait. No message was sent or received, so she apparently went under too fast to get a message out. Two days later, searching vessels found wreckage that was the remains of her and her 94 crewmen.

In December, U-boats made more reckless attacks, sinking a Liberty ship just outside Halifax Harbor on the 21st. On the 24th, they sank the minesweeper *Clayoquot* and the two corvettes with her picked up an acoustic torpedo apiece in their CAT gear.

On the 27th, news was received that the Canadian corvettes *St. Thomas* and *Edmundston* had sunk a U-boat in mid-Atlantic, which was some satisfaction, but was still no cause for jubilation within the escort force.

At the end of 1944, the Canadian Navy had sixty frigates and corvettes on the Mid-Ocean run alone. Another forty-five were organized as the Western Escort Force, seventeen corvettes and fourteen Bangors were in the Channel, and over ninety older vessels in the Local Escort Force.

In February 1945, the U-boats switched back to the mid-Atlantic. Eleven submarines were sunk that month, versus five Allied naval ships. One of those was the Canadian corvette *Trentonian*.

On 22 February, during the early afternoon, she was escorting a convoy eastward a few miles off Falmouth. At 13:20 hours, with no previous warning, a torpedo struck the second ship in the port column. *Trentonian*, which had been doing forward sweeps, immediately came about and started an Asdic sweep. The merchantman had been torpedoed on the starboard side, and since the corvette was on the port side of the convoy, she had to thread her way through the columns of ships to reach the suspected site.

Just as she cleared the lines of merchantmen, a torpedo struck her astern, slewing her around and flooding the engine room. Within four minutes the stern began to settle, and the crew were ordered to abandon ship. Hardly had the last man gotten over the side, when the corvette upended and sank in moments. Casualties numbered six dead, eleven wounded. The U-boat was never contacted again, although she was searched for most diligently.

Suddenly, on 8 May, at 22:01 hours, the German High Command called on all U-boats to surface, report their position, and surrender to the nearest Allied warship or base. The U-boat war was over! The signal was repeated every two hours for the next three weeks.

But the corvettes were still to escort convoys through May and June. In mid-May the Channel corvettes began to disband. *Mayflower* and *Snowberry*, although Canadian manned, reverted to their British owners on 21 May. *Baddeck* sailed for Canada on 24 May, and by 15 June all the corvettes were on their way home. It was a time of mingled sadness and relief that they had survived. I believe that Jim Lamb summed it up best in *Corvette Navy:*

". . .England. . .The whole command

"K is for corvette"—and boy could they roll! Some swore they could roll on wet grass, but despite their lively movement, they were excellent sea-keeping vessels, surviving storms that broke up larger vessels. Here, HMCS EYEBRIGHT corkscrews down a quartering sea, as two crew members watch the rudder and propeller in disbelief. 27 October 1941. [Public Archives of Canada]

HMCS EYEBRIGHT, May 1943. Note she is cork-screwing as the bows prepare to plunge. Ship is overall off-white with light Admiralty Disruptive pattern, with medium grey over off-white. The oblong box immediately ahead of the bandstand is a shelter for the stern look-out, who walks the bandstand. [Public Archives of Canada]

HMCS ST. THOMAS in late 1944. This Castle Class corvette is painted in an off-white, with Admiralty Disruptive pattern in medium gray. The odd pattern is startlingly evident. The three Maple leaves signify she is with C3 Escort Group. [Ken MacPherson]

Shows HMCS COBURG in 1944 in the St. Lawrence River. Note the split hedgehog cabinets on either side of the bridge, on the gun platform. Colors are medium gray over off-white. [Public Archives of Canada]

HMCS TRENTONIAN as she appeared in 1944, prior to her sinking. British Admiralty Disruptive in light gray/medium grey. Censor has removed pennant number. She was involved with the cable-layer, ST. MARGARET, when she was shelled by an American destroyer. She and ST. MARGARET were quarantined upon return to port until the news could be suppressed. [Ken MacPherson]

HMCS LA CHUTE. Although not involved with the Channel war, she was active in the North Atlantic. This shows a 1944 Western Approaches paint scheme, as well as the normal hedghog. Note the flair and rake of the bows to early corvettes. [Ken MacPherson]

HMCS BRANDON in 1942, with a classic Western Approaches scheme, SW2 antenna, and widened bridge with 20 mm Oerlikons. [Author's collection]

HMCS CHICOUTIMI in 1943, with an interesting three-color Admiralty Disruptive scheme of off-white, dark green, and medium gray or dark blue. [Marcom]

How it all ended. Here in the gym at HMCS STADACONA (now CFB Halifax) ratings and petty officers queue up doing their 'Out Routine' which will make them civilians again after six years of service life for some of them. A sad and glad time for most, with an uncertain time ahead. [Marcom]

The model of HMCS VILLE DE QUEBEC that resides in the Maritime Museum on Citadel Hill in Halifax. This model is accurate in scale and shows her in a two-color Western Approaches scheme, the dark angular portions being a robin's egg blue. Overall color is off-white, with very realistic rust streaking. This is how she looked in 1942-1943, before refit. [Author's collection]

was running down; its bases were being closed, its ships released to other commands, and its men were queuing up for demobilization. Leave-taking at Londonderry was like a wake; one hardly knew whether to laugh or to cry. We crossed the Atlantic for the last time, with all our lights blazing; the first — and last — time we did so.

"We bid Newfyjohn a last, long farewell; already its South Side jetties seemed forlorn, for the mid-ocean types had already taken their departure, and there were few familiar faces left around. We fueled and backed off into that crowded little harbour for the last time, the three blasts of our siren echoing off the bare hills we had known so well. We took our last look at the pleasant little jerry-built wooden city we had come to love, and where we had so many friends; in the late afternoon sunshine, the homely buildings glowed warmly, and there seemed not one that did not have some meaning and significance to each of us. We could even make out the rickety staircase leading to the Crowsnest, scene of so many happy hours. It was with a heavy heart that we took old *Camrose* down the harbour she had known so long and so well, cleared the entrance and stood out past Cape Spear's storm-battered light house. . ."

Camrose, a good example of demobilization of men and ships, proceeded to Halifax, where she lost her crew and stores:

". . .we moved her across the harbour, first, where working parties from the shore removed her ammunition and depth charges, her Asdic and other technical equipment, and specialized fighting gear of every kind. When they had done and had gone their way, we raised steam and took her away on her last voyage. . . Sydney in Cape Breton was our first stop; we went alongside the great cranes there and had our Oerlikons and four-inch mounting, our surface main armament, lifted out of the ship. Poor old *Camrose*: for the first time she showed her years, a veritable toothless tiger; it was surprising what a difference the removal of her forward gun made in her appearance. We hoisted our long decommissioning pendant; *Camrose* was ready for her last voyage.

". . .Off Sorel we picked up our pilot, a voluble little French-Canadian chap, who guided us, with a torrent of orders and cautions and gestures through a channel into a cluster of reedy islands, among which we picked our way before emerging at our final destination.

"Ahead of us, a long stretch of water opened up, hemmed in by a featureless line of low swampy sandbars. And in that stretch, moored head to tail at rows of buoys, lay the entire corvette navy, together with the destroyers and frigates that had led the escort groups. There were hundreds of them, still in their sea-worn Western Approaches camouflage, but strangely altered. For one they had no guns; for another, there was not a sign of life. They were no longer ships, but mere lifeless hulks, the bare bones of once-great fighting ships, lying huddled in decaying ranks in this dismal place. We had arrived at the graveyard of the elephants."

FLOWER CLASS **1939-1940 PROGRAM**

NAME	BUILDER	COMMISSIONED	PAID OFF OR LOST
Agassiz	Burrard	23 January 1941	14 June 1945
Alberni	Yarrows	4 February 1941	21 August 1944*
Algoma	Port Arthur	11 July 1941	6 July 1945
Amherst	St. John	5 August 1941	7 November 1945
Arrowhead	Marine Industries	22 November 1940	27 June 1945
Arvida	Morton	22 May 1941	14 June 1945
Baddeck	Davie	18 May 1941	4 July 1945
Barrie	Collingwood	12 May 1941	26 June 1945
Battleford	Collingwood	31 July 1941	18 July 1945
Bittersweet	Marine Industries	23 January 1941	22 June 1945
Brandon	Davie	22 July 1941	22 June 1945
Buctouche	Davie	5 June 1941	15 June 1945
Camrose	Marine Industries	30 June 1941	18 July 1945
Chambly	Vickers	18 December 1940	20 June 1945
Chicoutimi	Vickers	12 May 1941	16 June 1945
Chilliwack	Burrard	8 April 1941	14 July 1945
Cobalt	Port Arthur	25 November 1940	17 June 1945
Collingwood	Collingwood	9 November 1940	23 July 1945
Dauphin	Vickers	17 May 1941	20 June 1945
Dawson	Victoria	6 October 1941	19 June 1945
Drumheller	Collingwood	13 September 1941	5 July 1945
Dunvegan	Marine Industries	9 September 1941	3 July 1945
Edmunston	Yarrows	21 October 1941	16 June 1945
Eyebright	Vickers	26 November 1940	17 June 1945
Fennel	Marine Industries	15 January 1941	12 June 1945
Galt	Collingwood	15 May 1941	21 June 1945
Hepatica	Davie	12 November 1940	27 June 1945
Kamloops	Victoria	17 March 1941	27 June 1945
Kamsack	Port Arthur	4 October 1941	22 July 1945
Kenogami	Port Arthur	29 June 1941	9 July 1945
Lethbridge	Vickers	25 June 1941	23 July 1945
Levis	G.T. Davie	16 May 1941	19 September 1941*
Louisburg	Morton	20 October 1941	6 February 1943*
Lunenburg	G.T. Davie	4 December 1941	23 July 1945
Matapedia	Morton	9 May 1941	16 June 1945
Mayflower	Vickers	28 November 1940	31 May 1945 returned
Moncton	St. John	24 April 1942	12 December 1945
Moosejaw	Collingwood	19 June 1941	8 July 1945
Morden	Port Arthur	6 September 1941	29 June 1945
Nanaimo	Yarrows	26 April 1941	28 September 1945
Napenee	Kingston	12 May 1941	12 July 1945
Oakville	Port Arthur	18 November 1941	16 July 1945
Orillia	Collingwood	25 November 1940	2 July 1945
Pictou	Davie	29 April 1941	12 July 1945
Prescott	Kingston	26 June 1941	20 July 1945
Quesnel	Victoria	23 May 1941	3 July 1945
Rimouski	Davie	26 April 1941	24 July 1945
Rosthern	Port Arthur	17 June 1941	19 July 1945
Sackville	St. John	30 December 1941	Retained
Saskatoon	Vickers	9 June 1941	25 June 1945
Shawinigan	G.T. Davie	19 September 1941	24 November 1944*
Shediac	Davie	8 July 1941	28 August 1945
Sherbrooke	Marine Industries	5 June 1941	28 June 1945
Snowberry	Davie	30 November 1940	8 June 1945 returned
Sorel	Marine Industries	19 August 1941	22 June 1945

NAME	BUILDER	COMMISSIONED	PAID OFF OR LOST
Spikenard	Davie	8 December 1940	10 February 1942*
Sudbury	Kingston	15 October 1941	28 August 1945
Summerside	Morton	11 September 1941	6 July 1945
The Pas	Collingwood	21 October 1941	24 July 1945
Trail	Burrard	30 April 1941	17 July 1945
Trillium	Vickers	31 October 1940	27 June 1945 returned
Wetaskiwin	Burrard	16 December 1940	19 June 1945
Weyburn	Port Arthur	26 November 1941	22 February 1943*
Windflower	Davie	26 October 1940	7 December 1941*

NOTES

As can be seen by the delivery dates on most of the 1939-40 program, delays of materials, lack of trained workers and insufficient facilities delayed production for up to a year in some cases. But when deliveries started, there were shortages in crew.

These corvettes were basically the same as Admiralty models, with only minor differences. One was the bandstand was moved aft to the end of the deckhouse and the galley shifted foreward abaft the bridge. The first fourteen were to Admiralty specifications. Main armament was, at first, a Mk. IX BL 4 inch, later a Massey-Harris 4 inch as Canadian industry caught up with the demand. A two-pounder (40 mm) Vickers pom-pom was eventually fitted in the bandstand, but because of shortages, 2 × 1 Browning .5 machine guns or Vickers .303 were fitted as temporary anti-aircraft mounts. Lewis guns were fitted to the bridge wings.

Specifications for all programs (except where noted)

Displacement (other than Revised Flower Class): 950 tons
Overall Length (same exception): 205 feet 1 inch
Extreme Breadth (beam)—all classes: 33 feet 1 inch
Draught Forward (other than Revised Flower Class): 8 feet 3 inches
Draught Aft (same exception): 13 feet 5 inches (both full load)
Engines (all classes: steam reciprocating, triple expansion, I.H.P. 2,800 = 16 knots
Boilers: two drum-type in early corvettes, two water-tube type in later units
Forecastle of this program run were lengthened at later dates except: Alberni, Weyburn, Chicoutimi, Levis, Louisburg, Nanaimo, Rosthern, Shawinigan, The Pas, Spikenard, and Windflower.
Endurance: 3,450 miles at 12 knots

FLOWER CLASS **1940-41 PROGRAM**

Dundas	Victoria Mach.	1 April 1942	17 July 1945
Brantford	Midland	15 May 1942	17 August 1945
Midland	Midland	8 November 1941	15 July 1945
New Westminster	Victoria Mach.	31 January 1942	21 June 1945
Timmins	Yarrows	10 February 1942	15 July 1945
Vancouver	Yarrows	20 March 1942	26 June 1945

NOTES

As per specifications for previous program, except water-tube boilers fitted. All had the extended foc'scule in construction, except Brantford.

REVISED FLOWER CLASS **1940-41 Program**

Calgary	Marine Industries	16 December 1941	19 June 1945
Charlottetown	Kingston	13 December 1941	11 September 1942*
Fredericton	Marine Industries	8 December 1941	14 July 1945
Halifax	Collingwood	26 November 1941	12 July 1945
Kitchener	G.T. Davie	28 June 1942	11 July 1945
LaMalbaie	Marine Industries	28 April 1942	28 June 1945
Port Arthur	Port Arthur	26 May 1942	11 July 1945
Regina	Marine Industries	22 January 1942	11 September 1945
Ville de Quebec	Morton	24 May 1942	6 July 1945
Woodstock	Collingwood	1 May 1942	retained—sold 18 Mar. 1946

NOTES
Displacement for this program only: 1,015 tons
Overall Length: 208 feet 4 inches
Draught Forward: 11 feet
Draught Aft: 15 feet 7 inches (both full load)
Built with increased shear and flare in the bow and lengthened forecastle. No change in other specifications. Foremast stepped aft of bridge in this class to improve forward vision. Oerlikons added to extended bridge wings.

REVISED FLOWER CLASS (Increased Endurance) 1942-43 Program

Athol	Morton	14 October 1943	17 July 1945
Coburg	Midland	11 May 1944	16 June 1945
Fergus	Collingwood	18 November 1944	14 July 1945
Frontenac	Kingston	26 October 1943	22 July 1945
Guelph	Collingwood	9 May 1944	27 June 1945
Hawkesbury	Morton	14 June 1944	10 July 1945
Lindsay	Midland	15 November 1943	18 July 1945
Louisburg II	Morton	13 December 1943	25 June 1945
Norsyd	Morton	22 December 1943	25 June 1945
North Bay	Collingwood	25 October 1943	1 July 1945
Owen Sound	Collingwood	17 November 1943	19 July 1945
Riviere du Loup	Morton	21 November 1943	2 July 1945
St. Lambert	Morton	27 May 1944	20 July 1945
Trentonian	Kingston	1 December 1943	22 January 1945*
Whitby	Midland	6 June 1944	16 July 1945

NOTES
Same as others, but increased rake to bow is highly noticeable. Draught and endurance greater over the original Flower.
Draught Forward: 11 feet 5 inches
Draught Aft: 16 feet
Endurance increased through additional tanks to 7,400 miles at 10 knots to be better able to contend with the Newfie to 'Derry run.
Length: 208 feet 4 inches

REVISED FLOWER CLASS (Increased Endurance) 1943-44 Program

Asbestos	Morton	16 June 1944	8 July 1945
Beauharnois	Morton	25 September 1944	12 July 1945
Belleville	Kingston	19 October 1944	5 July 1945
Lachute	Morton	26 October 1944	10 July 1945
Merritonia	Morton	10 November 1944	11 July 1945
Parry Sound	Midland	30 August 1944	10 July 1945
Peterborough	Kingston	1 June 1944	19 July 1945
Smith's Falls	Kingston	28 November 1944	8 July 1945
Stellarton	Morton	29 September 1944	1 July 1945
Strathroy	Midland	20 November 1944	12 July 1945
Thorlock	Midland	13 November 1944	15 July 1945
West York	Midland	6 October 1944	9 July 1945

NOTES
Displacement was 970 tons over the original 940 of the first program. This was the last Flower of the Flower Class corvettes, as the design had been superceded by better vessels, such as frigates. As can be noted, losses dropped steadily in the last two programs, with only one loss. Improved air cover, better and more convoy escort screens, hunter-killer groups, plus the invasion of France and loss of the Channel ports had diminished the U-boat threat greatly.

FOREIGN BUILT CORVETTES

REVISED FLOWER CLASS (Increased Endurance)
Same as 1943-44 Revised Flower (increased Endurance)

Forest Hill	Ferguson Brothers	1 December 1943	9 July 1945

Giffard	Alex Hall	10 November 1943	5 July 1945
Long Branch	John Brown	5 January 1944	17 June 1945
Mimico	John Brown	8 February 1944	18 July 1945

NOTES
These were British-ordered, but given to the RCN. All were disposed of by Crown Assets Disposal Corporation, along with the majority of Canadian units.

CASTLE CLASS CORVETTES

Arnprior	Harland & Wolff	8 June 1944	14 March 1946
Bowmanville	Wm. Pickersgill	28 September 1944	15 February 1946
Copper Cliff	Blythe Dry Docks	25 July 1944	21 November 1945
Hespeler	Henry Robb	28 February 1944	15 November 1945
Humberstone	A & J Inglis	6 September 1944	17 November 1945
Huntsville	Fleming & Ferguson	6 June 1944	15 February 1946
Kincardine	Smith's Dock Company	19 June 1944	27 February 1946
Leaside	Smith's Dock Company	21 August 1944	16 November 1945
Orangeville	Henry Robb	24 April 1944	12 April 1946
Petrolia	Harland & Wolff	29 June 1944	8 March 1946
St. Thomas	Smith's Dock Company	4 May 1944	22 November 1945
Tillsonburg	Ferguson Brothers	29 June 1944	15 February 1946

NOTES
Displacement: 1,060 tons
Overall Length: 251 feet 9 inches
Extreme Beam: 36 feet 8 inches
Maximum Draught: 15 feet 5 inches
Boilers: two Admiralty three-drum type, triple expansion engine
Full Speed: 16.5 knots
Endurance: 6,200 nautical miles at 15 knots
Most noticeable about this class were increased size, lattice mast, sharply raked bow section, squared stern. These were all originally ordered by Admiralty, but were traded to the RCN for minesweepers, which were needed more by the RN. This was the largest corvette built and saw only limited action. All were sold or scrapped.

* = sunk in action

SHAWINIGAN, high-speed trials late in 1941, after commissioning at Davie Shipyard. Overall medium gray. Note the lack of a gun shield, but mainmast has been deleted. [Public Archives of Canada]

COMMANDING OFFICERS OF CANADIAN CORVETTES 1939-1945

SHIP	'K' NUMBER	COMMANDING OFFICER	FROM	TO
AGASSIZ	K-129	Lt. B.D.D. Johnson, RCNR	23 January 1941	14 March 1943
		Lt.Cdr. E.M. Moore, RCNR	15 March 1943	13 May 1944
		Lt. F.E. Burrows, RCNVR	14 May 1944	5 May 1945
		Lt. G.C. Thomas, RCNVR	6 May 1945	12 June 1945
ALBERNI	K-103	Lt.Cdr. G.O. Baugh, OBE, RCNR	6 January 1941	11 October 1942
		Lt. I.H. Bell, RCNVR	12 October 1942	21 August 1944
ALGOMA	K-127	Lt. J. Harding, RCNR	26 May 1941	14 October 1943
		Lt. E.R. Hyman, RCNVR	15 October 1943	4 April 1944
		Lt. S.B. Kelly, RCNVR	5 April 1944	5 April 1944
		Lt. L.F. Moore, RCNR	6 April 1944	24 August 1944
		Lt. J.N. Finlayson, RCNR	25 August 1944	2 July 1945
AMHERST	K-148	Lt.Cdr. A.K. Young, RCNR	6 February 1941	20 November 1941
		Lt. H.G. Denyer, RCNR	21 November 1941	19 September 1942
		Lt. L.C. Audette, RCNVR	20 September 1942	24 May 1944
		Lt. D.M. Fraser, RCNVR	25 May 1944	16 December 1944
		Lt. K.W. Winsby, RCNVR	17 December 1944	11 July 1945
ARNPRIOR	K-494	Lt. S.D. Thom, RCNVR	8 June 1944	2 September 1945
ARROWHEAD	K-145	Lt. V. Torraville, RCN	21 November 1940	17 January 1941
		Lt.Cdr. E.G. Skinner, RCNR	18 January 1941	25 March 1942
		Skpr.Lt. L.A. Hickey, RCNR	26 March 1942	21 October 1944
		Lt. R.H. Sylvester, RCNVR	22 October 1944	27 June 1945
ARVIDA	K-113	Lt. A.I. MacKay, RCNR	1 November 1940	6 August 1942
		Lt. D.G. King, RCNVR	7 August 1942	25 November 1943
		Lt. J.C.P. Desrochers, RCNVR	26 November 1943	15 March 1944
		Lt. D.W.G. Storey, RCNVR	16 March 1944	10 June 1945
ATHOLL	K-15	Lt. W.D.H. Gardiner, RCNVR	14 October 1943	12 July 1945
ASBESTOS	K-358	Lt. J. Cuthbert, RCNR	24 April 1944	4 July 1945
BADDECK	K-147	Lt. A.H. Easton, RCNR	18 May 1941	5 April 1942
		Lt. F.W. Thompson, RCNVR	6 April 1942	20 April 1942
		Lt. L.G. Cumming, RCNVR	21 April 1942	5 October 1942
		Lt. J. Brock, RCNVR	6 October 1942	17 August 1943
		Lt. D.H. Fozer, RCNVR	18 August 1943	17 October 1943
		Lt. G.C. Brown, RCNVR	18 October 1943	15 June 1944
		Lt. C.R. Campbell, RCNVR	16 June 1944	19 June 1944
		Lt.Cdr. F.G. Hutchings, RCNR	20 June 1944	29 June 1945
BARRIE	K-138	Lt. R.M. Mosher, RCNR	12 May 1941	9 January 1942
		Ch.Skpr. G.N. Downey, RCNR	10 January 1942	28 March 1942
		Lt. R.M. Mosher, RCNR	29 March 1942	13 March 1943
		Lt. H.O. Magill, RCNVR	14 March 1943	8 October 1943
		Lt. D.R. Watson, RCNR	9 October 1943	15 June 1944
		Lt. W.D. Stokvis, RCNVR	16 June 1944	22 June 1945
BATTLEFORD	K-165	Lt. R.J. Roberts, RCNR	31 July 1941	31 August 1942
		Lt. F.A. Beck, RCNVR	1 September 1942	25 June 1943
		Lt. H.H. Turnbull, RCNVR	26 June 1943	19 June 1944
		Lt. P.A.F. Lanlois, RCNVR	20 June 1944	12 May 1945
BEAUHARNOIS	K-540	Lt. E.C. Smith, RCNVR	1 August 1944	20 May 1945
		Lt. J.M. Pretty, RCNVR	21 May 1945	6 July 1945
BELLEVILLE	K-332	Lt. J.E. Korning, RCNVR	18 October 1944	6 May 1945
		Lt.Cdr. R.M. Powell, RCNVR	7 May 1945	30 June 1945
BITTERSWEET	K-182	Lt.Cdr. J.A. Woods, RCNR	1 November 1940	30 November 1942
		Lt. F.B. Brooks-Hill, RCNVR	1 December 1942	9 July 1944
		Lt. F.W. Bogardus, RCNVR	10 July 1944	7 December 1944

SHIP	'K' NUMBER	COMMANDING OFFICER	FROM	TO
		Lt. B. Sangster, RCNVR	8 December 1944	16 December 1944
		Skpr.Lt. F.C. Smith, RCNR	17 December 1944	22 June 1945
BOWMANVILLE	K-493	Lt.Cdr. M.S. Duffin, RCNVR	28 September 1944	2 September 1945
BRANDON	K-149	Lt. J.C. Littler, RCNR	22 July 1941	24 November 1942
		Lt. H.E. McArthur, RCNVR	25 November 1942	25 April 1944
		Lt. J.F. Evans, RCNVR	26 April 1944	26 April 1945
		Lt. P.J. Lawrence, RCNR	27 April 1945	20 June 1945
BRANTFORD	K-218	Lt. W.D.F. Jackson, RCNR	15 May 1942	26 April 1943
		Lt. J.A.R. Allan, RCNVR	27 April 1943	17 August 1943
		Lt. R.C. Eaton, RCNVR	18 August 1943	28 September 1944
		Lt. J.P. Kieran, RCNR	29 September 1944	27 April 1945
		Lt. R.M. Smillie, RCNVR	28 April 1945	17 August 1945
BUCTOUCHE	K-179	Lt. W.W. Mackney, RCNR	5 June 1941	6 May 1942
		Skpr.Lt. G.N. Downey, RCNR	7 May 1942	4 August 1943
		Skpr.Lt. H.E. Young, RCNR	5 August 1943	4 December 1944
		Skpr.Lt. E.S.N. Pleasance, RCNR	5 December 1944	4 February 1945
		Skpr.Lt. E.L. Ritchie, RCNR	5 February 1945	12 June 1945
CALGARY	K-231	Lt. G. Lancaster, RCNR	15 December 1941	19 June 1942
		Lt. H.K. Hill, RCNVR	20 June 1942	21 June 1943
		Lt. G.M. Orr, RCNVR	22 June 1943	12 August 1943
		Lt. R.B. Bush, RCNVR	13 August 1943	17 March 1944
		Lt. A.A.R. Dykes, RCNR	18 March 1944	15 September 1944
		Lt. L.D.M. Saunders, RCNVR	16 September 1944	12 June 1945
CAMROSE	K-154	Lt. L.R. Pavillard, RCNR	30 June 1941	24 November 1944
		Lt. J.B. Lamb, RCNVR	25 November 1944	18 July 1945
CHAMBLY	K-116	Lt. E.T. Simmonds, RCNVR	3 December 1940	17 December 1940
		Lt.Cdr. F.C. Smith, RCNR	18 December 1940	25 March 1941
		Cdr. J.D. Prentice, RCN	26 March 1941	5 September 1942
		Lt. A.F. Pickard, RCNR	6 September 1942	26 January 1944
		Lt. S.D. Taylor, RCNR	27 January 1944	22 June 1944
		Lt. H.A. Ovenden, RCNR	23 June 1944	28 April 1945
		Lt.Cdr. J.B.B. Shaw, RCN	29 April 1945	15 June 1945
CHARLOTTETOWN	K-244	Lt. J.W. Bonner, RCNR	12 December 1941	11 September 1942
CHICOUTIMI	K-156	Lt. William Black, RCNR	10 April 1941	10 May 1942
		Lt. H.G. Dupont, RCNR	11 May 1942	8 January 1943
		Lt.Cdr. J.F. Stairs, RCNVR	9 January 1943	8 August 1943
		Lt. F. Cross, RCNR	9 August 1943	3 September 1944
		Lt. A.F. Giffin, RCNVR	4 September 1944	14 June 1945
CHILLIWACK	K-131	Lt. L.F. Foxall, RCNR	8 April 1941	25 May 1943
		Lt.Cdr. C.R. Coughlin, RCNVR	26 May 1943	11 April 1944
		Lt. D.R. Watson, M.B.E., RCNR	12 April 1944	9 July 1945
COBALT	K-124	Lt.Cdr. R.B. Campbell, RCN	10 September 1940	19 May 1941
		Lt. C.J. Angus, RCNR	20 May 1941	5 May 1943
		Lt. R.A. Judges, RCNVR	6 May 1943	30 March 1944
		Lt. A.W. Bett, G.M., RCNR	31 March 1944	25 June 1944
		Lt.Cdr. R.M. Wallace, RCNVR	26 June 1944	15 June 1945
COBURG	K-333	Lt. G.H. Johnson, RCNVR	20 March 1944	10 June 1945
COLLINGWOOD	K-180	Lt. N.G. Bennett, RCNR	10 September 1940	16 April 1941
		Lt. W. Woods, RCNR	17 April 1941	9 December 1942
		Lt. D.W. Goos, RCN	10 December 1942	16 May 1943
		Lt.Cdr. R.J.C. Pringle, RCNVR	17 May 1943	2 January 1944
		Lt. H.R. Knight, RCNR	3 January 1944	2 May 1945
		Lt.Cdr. E.B. Pearce, RCNVR	3 May 1945	19 July 1945
COPPERCLIFF	K-495	Lt. A.D. Ritchie, RCNVR	19 April 1944	25 July 1944
		Lt.Cdr. F.G. Hutchings, RCNR	26 July 1944	2 September 1945

SHIP	'K' NUMBER	COMMANDING OFFICER	FROM	TO
DAUPHIN	K-157	Lt. R.A.S. McNeil, O.B.E., RCNR	12 April 1941	17 January 1943
		Lt. M.H. Wallace, RCNR	18 January 1943	10 October 1944
		Lt. E.R. O'Kelly, RCNVR	11 October 1944	6 May 1945
		Lt. G.R. Brassard, RCNVR	7 May 1945	16 June 1945
DAWSON	K-104	Lt. A.H.G. Storrs, RCNR	6 October 1941	7 June 1943
		Lt.Cdr. T.S.P. Ryan, O.B.E., RCNR	8 June 1943	30 March 1944
		Skpr.Lt. J.B. Cooper, RCNR	31 March 1944	15 June 1945
DRUMHELLER	K-167	Lt.Cdr. G.H. Griffiths, RCN	13 September 1941	15 October 1942
		Lt. L.P. Denny, RCNR	16 October 1942	20 August 1943
		Lt.Cdr. A.H.G. Storrs, RCNR	21 August 1943	27 December 1943
		Lt. H.R. Beck, RCNR	28 December 1943	5 July 1945
DUNDAS	K-229	Lt. R.W. Draney, RCNR	13 March 1942	17 May 1943
		Lt. R.W. Hart, RCNVR	18 May 1943	1 March 1944
		Lt. R.B. Taylor, RCNVR	2 March 1944	17 February 1945
		Lt. D.E. Howard, RCNVR	18 February 1945	13 May 1945
DUNVEGAN	K-177	Lt. J.C. Pratt, RCNVR	10 May 1941	22 May 1941
		Lt. J.A. Tullis, RCNR	23 May 1941	25 January 1943
		Lt. S.A. Burris, RCNR	26 January 1943	5 July 1944
		Lt. J.A. Rankin, RCNR	6 July 1944	11 March 1945
		Lt.Cdr. R.L.B. Hunter, RCNVR	12 March 1945	28 June 1945
EDMUNDSTON	K-106	Lt. R.D. Barrett, RCNR	21 October 1941	21 May 1944
		Lt. J. Leky, RCNVR	22 May 1944	12 June 1945
EYEBRIGHT	K-150	Lt. E. Randell, RCNR	1 November 1940	25 November 1940
		Lt. H.C.R. Davis, RCNR	26 November 1940	27 December 1942
		Lt. H.L. Quinn, RCNVR	28 December 1942	1 September 1944
		Lt. R.J. Margesson, RCNVR	2 September 1944	9 January 1945
		S/Lt. P.A. Lefroy, RCNVR	10 January 1945	17 June 1945
FENNEL	K-194	Lt.Cdr. J.N. Smith, RCNR	1 November 1940	31 October 1941
		Lt. J.M. Gillison, RCNR	1 November 1941	26 May 1942
		Lt. R.B. Warwick, RCNVR	27 May 1942	5 September 1943
		Lt.Cdr. W.P. Moffat, RCN	6 September 1943	15 May 1944
		Lt.Cdr. K.L. Johnson, RCNVR	16 May 1944	12 June 1945
FERGUS	K-334	Lt. H.F. Farncomb, RCNVR	24 October 1944	9 July 1945
FOREST HILL	K-360	Lt. E.J. Jones, RCNR	1 December 1943	5 July 1945
FREDERICTON	K-245	Lt.Cdr. J.H.S. MacDonald, RCNR	15 November 1941	17 February 1942
		Lt. J.E. Harrington, RCNVR	18 February 1942	20 July 1944
		Lt. J.C. Smyth, RCNR	21 July 1944	29 July 1945
FRONTENAC	K-335	Lt. E.T.F. Wennberg, RCNVR	26 October 1943	15 March 1945
		Lt. D.R. Baker, RCNVR	16 March 1945	17 July 1945
GIFFARD	K-275	Lt.Cdr. C. Peterson, RCNR	30 October 1943	9 May 1944
		Lt. G.H. Matheson, RCNR	10 May 1944	30 June 1945
GUELPH	K-687	Lt. G.H. Hayes, DSC, RCNR	13 March 1944	14 May 1945
		Lt. F.D. Wickett, RCNVR	15 May 1945	23 June 1945
GALT	K-163	Lt. A.D. Landles, RCNR	10 April 1941	9 March 1942
		Lt. A.M. Kirkpatrick, RCNVR	10 March 1942	9 August 1943
		Lt. E.P. Taylor, RCNVR	10 August 1943	24 April 1945
		Lt. J.C. Lorriman, RCNVR	25 April 1945	19 June 1945
HALIFAX	K-237	Lt.Cdr. Copeland, OBE, RCNR	15 November 1941	6 February 1943
		Lt. M.F. Oilver, RCNR	7 February 1943	21 June 1944
		Lt.Cdr. R.M. Hanbury, RCNVR	22 June 1944	3 September 1944
		Lt. L.E. Horne, RCNVR	4 September 1944	10 July 1945
HAWKESBURY	K-415	Lt. W.G. Curry, RCNVR	20 March 1944	7 July 1945

SHIP	'K' NUMBER			
HEPATICA	K-159	Lt. C. Copelin, RCNR	27 August 1940	31 October 1941
		Lt. T. Gilmour, RCNR	1 November 1941	11 April 1943
		Lt. H.E. Lade, RCNR	12 April 1943	5 September 1943
		Lt. J.A. Ferguson, RCNR	6 September 1943	4 November 1944
		Lt. E.M. Lutes, RCNVR	5 November 1944	27 June 1945
HESPELER	K-489	Lt.Cdr. N.S.C. Dickson, RCNVR	28 February 1944	13 November 1944
		Lt. G.F. Manning, RCNVR	14 November 1944	2 September 1945
HUMBERSTONE	K-497	Lt.Cdr. A. Boucher, RCNVR	not known	5 September 1944
		Lt. G.C. MacDonald, RCNVR	6 September 1944	2 September 1945
HUNTSVILLE	K-499	Lt. C.B. Hermann, RCNVR	10 April 1944	— September 1945
KAMLOOPS	K-176	Lt. J.M. Gillison, RCNR	17 March 1941	31 October 1941
		Lt. P.J.B. Watts, RCNR	1 November 1941	4 February 1942
		Lt. I.W. McTavish, RCNR	5 February 1942	1 March 1942
		Lt. D.M. Stewart, RCNR	2 March 1942	27 March 1942
		Lt.Cdr. J.H. Marshall, RCNVR	28 March 1942	22 August 1942
		Lt. N.S.C. Dickinson, RCNVR	23 August 1942	28 September 1942
		Lt. P.R. Gillis, RCNVR	29 September 1942	— July 1945
KAMSACK	K-171	Lt. E. Randall, RCNR	4 October 1941	1 March 1943
		Lt. D.M. Stewart, RCNR	2 March 1943	17 March 1943
		Lt.Cdr. W.C. Halliday, RCNR	18 March 1943	4 May 1945
		Lt.Cdr. R.F. Wilson, RCNVR	5 May 1945	to payoff
KENOGAMI	K-125	Lt.Cdr. R. Jackson, RCNVR	8 May 1941	2 August 1942
		Lt. R.G. McKenzie, RCNVR	3 August 1942	21 November 1942
		Lt. J.L. Percy, RCNVR	22 November 1942	5 July 1945
KINCARDINE	K-490	Lt. R.P. Brown, RCNVR	19 June 1944	payoff June 1945
KITCHENER	K-225	Lt. W. Evans, RCNVR	28 June 1942	16 January 1944
		Lt. J.E. Moles, RCNVR	17 January 1944	5 July 1945
LACHUTE	K-440	Lt. R.G. Hatrick, RCNVR	25 September 1944	6 July 1945
LAMALBAIE	K-273	Lt. Ian W. MacTavish, RCNR	5 February 1942	11 February 1943
		Lt. James S. Davis, RCNVR	12 February 1943	7 June 1944
		Lt. Ernest F. Piper, RCNVR	8 June 1944	21 February 1945
		Lt. Timothy H. Dunn, RCNVR	22 February 1945	2 July 1945
LEASIDE	K-492	Lt. G.G.K. Holder, RCNVR	3 July 1944	15 June 1945
		Lt. H. Brynjolfson, RCNVR	16 June 1945	paid-off same date
LETHBRIDGE	K-160	Lt. W. Mahan, RCNR	11 May 1941	24 June 1941
		Lt. H. Freeland, RCNR	25 June 1941	20 October 1942
		Lt.Cdr. R.S. Kelly, RCNR	21 October 1942	21 April 1943
		Lt.Cdr. W. Woods, RCNR	22 April 1943	22 April 1943
		Lt. J. Roberts, RCNVR	22 April 1943	15 June 1943
		Lt.Cdr. St.C. Balfour, RCNVR	16 June 1943	14 March 1944
		Lt. F.H. Finold, RCNVR	15 March 1944	17 March 1944
		Lt. J.W. Bessey, RCNVR	18 March 1944	7 May 1945
		Lt. J. Holland, RCNVR	8 May 1945	18 July 1945
LEVIS	K-115	Cdr. J.D. Prentice, RCN	18 November 1940	9 March 1941
		Lt. C.W. Gilding, RCNR	10 March 1941	19 September 1941
LINDSAY	K-338	Lt. G.A.V. Thomson, RCNVR	15 November 1943	14 July 1945
LONGBRANCH	K-487	Lt.Cdr. W.J. Kingsmill, RCNVR	5 January 1944	16 April 1944
		Lt.Cdr. R.J.G. Johnson, RCNVR	17 April 1944	7 October 1944
		Lt.Cdr. J.B. O'Brien, RCNVR	8 October 1944	21 February 1945
		Lt.Cdr. K.B. Culley, RCNVR	22 February 1945	14 June 1945
LOUISBURG	K-401	Lt.Cdr. W.F. Campbell, RCNVR	19 July 1941	6 February 1943
LOUISBURG (II)	K-401	Lt. J.B. Elmsley, RCNVR	12 December 1943	10 February 1945

SHIP	'K' NUMBER	COMMANDING OFFICER	FROM	TO
		Lt. M.W. Knowles, RCNVR	11 February 1945	21 June 1945
LUNENBURG	K-151	Lt. W.E. Harrison, RCNR	4 December 1941	10 October 1942
		Lt. D.L. Miller, DSC, RCNVR	11 October 1942	22 December 1944
		Lt. W.S. Thomson, RCNVR	23 December 1944	18 July 1945
MATAPEDIA	K-112	Lt. R.J. Herman, RCNR	9 May 1941	26 April 1943
		Lt. J.D. Frewer, RCNVR	27 April 1943	12 May 1944
		Lt. C.F. Usher, RCNVR	13 May 1944	14 June 1945
MAYFLOWER	K-191	Lt.Cdr. G.H. Stephen, RCNR	9 November 1940	12 May 1942
		Lt. V. Browne, RCNVR	13 May 1942	2 March 1944
		Lt. D.S. Martin, RCNR	3 March 1944	31 May 1945
MERRITTONIA	K-688	Lt. F.K. Ellis, RCNVR	10 November 1944	5 April 1945
		Lt.Cdr. J.F. Stairs, RCNVR	6 April 1945	6 May 1945
		Lt. R.J. Keelan, RCNVR	7 May 1945	5 July 1945
MIDLAND	K-220	Lt. A.B. Taylor, RCNR	8 November 1941	31 October 1943
		Lt. W.O. Barbour, RCNR	1 November 1943	11 July 1945
MIMICO	K-485	Lt. F.J. Jones, RCNVR	8 February 1944	14 February 1945
		Lt.Cdr. J.B. Elmsley, RCNVR	15 February 1945	13 May 1945
MONCTON	K-139	Lt. A.W. Ford, RCNR	12 October 1942	3 February 1944
		Lt.Cdr. A.T. Morrel, RCNR	4 February 1944	3 April 1944
		Lt.Cdr. R.J. Roberts, RCNR	4 April 1944	20 June 1944
		Lt. O.H.M. Wright, RCNVR	21 June 1944	26 January 1945
		Lt. W. McCombe, RCNR	27 January 1945	2 September 1945
MOOSEJAW	K-164	Lt. F.E. Grubb, RCN	19 June 1941	13 February 1942
		Lt. L.D. Quick, RCNR	14 February 1942	10 August 1943
		Lt. A. Harvey, RCNR	11 August 1943	13 March 1944
		Lt. H. Brynjolfson, RCNVR	14 March 1944	3 July 1945
MORDEN	K-170	Lt. J.J. Hodgkinson, RCNR	6 September 1941	2 June 1943
		Lt. E.C. Smith, RCNVR	3 June 1943	14 October 1943
		Lt. W. Turner, RCNR	15 October 1943	21 May 1944
		Lt. K.B. Culley, RCNVR	22 May 1944	18 February 1945
		Lt. F.D. Spindler, RCNVR	19 February 1945	25 June 1945
NANAIMO	K-101	Lt.Cdr. H.C.C. Daubeny, RCNR	26 April 1941	7 October 1941
		Lt. T.J. Bellas, —	8 October 1941	20 August 1942
		Lt.(N) E.U. Jones, RCNR	21 August 1942	10 October 1943
		Lt. J.E. Hastings, RCNR	11 October 1943	9 October 1944
		Lt. R.C. Eaton, RCNVR	10 October 1944	22 March 1945
		Lt.Cdr. W. Redford, RCNR	23 March 1945	28 August 1945
NAPANEE	K-118	Lt.Cdr. A.H. Hobson, RCNR	12 May 1941	5 December 1941
		Lt. S. Henderson, RCNR	6 Decmber 1941	10 June 1943
		Lt.Cdr. G.A. Powell, RCNVR	11 June 1943	6 July 1945
NEW WESTMINSTER	K-228	Lt.Cdr. R.G. McKenzie, RCNR	31 January 1942	19 June 1945
NORSYD	K-520	Lt. J.R. Biggs, RCNR	22 December 1943	20 October 1944
		Lt. W.P. Wickett, RCNVR	21 October 1944	21 June 1945
NORTH BAY	K-339	Lt.Cdr. B. Hynes, RCNVR	25 October 1943	23 January 1945
		Lt. J.W. Radford, RCNR	24 January 1945	18 February 1945
		Lt.Cdr. A.C. Campbell, RCNVR	19 February 1945	26 June 1945
OAKVILLE	K-178	Lt. A.C. Jones, RCNR	18 November 1941	11 May 1942
		Lt.Cdr. C.A. King, DSC, RCNR	12 May 1942	21 April 1943
		Lt. H.F. Farncomb, RCNVR	22 April 1943	22 October 1944
		Lt. M.A. Griffiths, RCNVR	23 October 1944	16 July 1945
ORANGEVILLE	K-491	Lt.Cdr. F.R. Pike, RCNVR	24 April 1944	2 September 1945
ORILLIA	K-119	Lt.Cdr. W.E.S. Briggs, RCNR	25 November 1940	4 September 1942

SHIP	'K' NUMBER	COMMANDING OFFICER	FROM	TO
		Lt. H.Y.W. Groos, RCNR	5 September 1942	13 February 1943
		Lt.Cdr. R. Jackson, RCNR	14 February 1943	16 April 1943
		Lt.Cdr. J.E. Mitchell, RCNVR	17 April 1943	7 May 1944
		Skpr.Lt. J.W. Sharpe, RCNR	8 May 1944	27 June 1945
OWEN SOUND	K-340	Lt.Cdr. J.M. Watson, RCNR	17 November 1943	13 April 1945
		Lt. F.H. Pinfold, RCNVR	14 April 1945	14 July 1945
PARRY SOUND	K-341	Lt.Cdr. W.J. Gilmore, RCNVR	30 August 1944	7 July 1945
PETERBOROUGH	K-342	Lt. J.B. Raine, RCNR	1 June 1944	14 July 1945
PETROLIA	K-498	Lt. P.W. Spragge, RCNVR	29 June 1944	10 November 1945
PICTOU	K-146	Lt. A.G.S. Griffin, —	20 April 1941	14 March 1943
		Lt. P.T. Byers	15 March 1943	19 November 1943
		Lt.Cdr. G.K. Fox, RCNVR	20 November 1943	1 October 1943
		Lt. F. Cross, RCNR	2 October 1943	29 June 1945
PORT ARTHUR	K-233	Lt. E.T. Simmons, DSC	26 May 1942	8 July 1943
		Lt.Cdr. K.T. Chisholm, RCNVR	9 July 1943	11 July 1945
PRESCOTT	K-161	Lt. H.A. Russell	26 June 1941	11 September 1942
		Lt.Cdr. W. McIsaac, RCNVR	12 September 1942	28 December 1944
		Lt. G.J. Mathewson, RCNVR	29 December 1944	17 July 1945
QUESNEL	K-133	Lt. J.A. Gow, —	23 May 1941	16 November 1942
		Lt. M. Smith, RCNR	17 November 1942	11 April 1943
		Lt. J.M. Laing, RCNR	12 April 1943	28 June 1945
RIMOUSKI	K-121	Lt. J.W. Bonner, RCNVR	27 April 1941	11 November 1941
		Lt.Cdr. A.G. Boulton, RCNVR	12 November 1941	1 December 1942
		Lt. R.J. Pickford, RCNVR	2 December 1942	13 April 1943
		Lt. C.D. Chivers, RCNVR	14 April 1943	17 December 1944
		Lt.Cdr. D.M. MacDonald, RCNVR	18 December 1944	19 July 1945
RIVIERE DU LOUP	K-357	Lt. R.N. Smillie, RCNVR	21 November 1943	22 January 1945
		Lt. R.D. Weldon, RCNVR	23 January 1945	27 June 1945
REGINA	K-234	Lt.Cdr. R.F. Harris, —	22 January 1942	23 February 1942
		Lt. R.S. Kelly	24 February 1942	20 October 1942
		Lt.Cdr. H. Freeland, —	21 October 1942	3 September 1943
		Lt. J.W. Radford, RCNR	4 September 1943	9 August 1944
ROSTHERN	K-169	Lt. W. Russell, —	17 June 1941	20 November 1941
		Cdr. P.B. Cross, —	21 November 1941	24 November 1942
		Lt.Cdr. R.J.G. Johnson, RCNVR	25 November 1942	1 February 1943
		Lt. S.R.P. Annett, RCNVR	2 February 1943	3 November 1944
		Lt.Cdr. R.F. Wilson, RCNVR	4 November 1944	6 April 1945
		Lt. D.R. Smythies, RCNVR	7 April 1945	16 July 1945
SASKATOON	K-158	Lt. F.J. Jones, —	9 June 1941	4 February 1942
		Lt.Cdr. C.A. King, DSC, RCNR	5 February 1942	14 February 1942
		Lt. J.S. Scott, —	15 February 1942	not known
		Lt. J.F. Evans, —	not known	9 July 1943
		Lt.Cdr. T. MacDuff, RCNR	10 July 1943	14 March 1944
		Lt.Cdr. R.S. Williams, RCNVR	15 March 1944	25 June 1945
SACKVILLE	K-181	Lt. W.R. Kirkland, —	30 December 1941	5 April 1942
		Lt. A.H. Easton, DSC, —	6 April 1942	9 April 1943
		Lt.Cdr. A.H. Rankin, RCNVR	10 April 1943	17 May 1944
		Lt. A.R. Hicks, RCNVR	18 May 1944	17 September 1944
		Lt. C.C. Love, RCNVR	18 September 1944	5 November 1944
		Lt. J.A. McKenna, RCNR	6 November 1944	2 September 1945
ST. LAMBERT	K-343	Lt. R.C. Hayden, RCNVR	27 July 1944	27 October 1944
		Lt.Cdr. W.D.H. Gardiner, RCNVR	27 October 1944	16 July 1945
ST. THOMAS	K-488	Lt.Cdr. L.P. Denny, RCNR	4 May 1944	26 January 1945

SHIP	'K' NUMBER			
		Lt.Cdr. B. Hynes, RCN	27 January 1945	20 June 1945
		Lt. J.B.K. Stewart, RCNVR	21 June 1945	22 November 1945
SHAWINIGAN	K-136	Lt.Cdr. C.P. Balfry, —	19 September 1941	4 January 1944
		Lt. R.S. Williams, RCNVR	4 January 1944	14 March 1944
		Lt. W.E. Callan, RCNVR	15 March 1944	4 June 1944
		Lt. W.J. Jones, RCNR	5 June 1944	24 November 1944
SHEDIAC	K-110	Lt. John E. Clayton, RCNR	8 July 1941	22 March 1943
		Lt.Cdr. A. Moorehouse, —	23 March 1943	9 February 1944
		Skpr.Lt. J.P. Cooper, RCNR	10 February 1944	30 March 1944
		Lt.Cdr. T.P. Ryan, OBE, RCNR	31 March 1944	31 July 1944
		Lt.Cdr. P.D. Taylor, —	1 August 1944	28 August 1945
SHERBROOKE	K-152	Lt.Cdr. E.G.M. Donald, —	5 June 1941	2 July 1942
		Lt. J.A.M. Levesque, RCNR	3 July 1942	29 August 1943
		Lt. R.A. Jarvis, RCNVR	29 August 1943	30 July 1944
		Lt. D.A. Binmore, RCNVR	31 July 1944	25 June 1945
SPIKENARD	K-198	Lt.Cdr. H.G. Shadforth, —	7 April 1941	10 February 1942
SMITH FALLS	K-345	Lt.Cdr. P.T. Byers, RCNR	28 November 1944	4 July 1945
SNOWBERRY	K-166	Lt. R.S. Kelley, —	30 November 1940	5 February 1942
		Lt.Cdr. P.J.B. Watts, —	6 February 1942	9 May 1943
		Lt. J.B. O'Brien, —	10 May 1943	9 November 1943
		Lt.Cdr. J.A. Dunn, RCNVR	10 November 1943	30 April 1945
		Lt. B.T.R. Russell, RCNR	1 May 1945	8 June 1945
SOREL	K-153	Lt. J.W. Dowling, —	19 August 1941	22 December 1941
		Lt. D.M. Cameron, —	23 December 1941	7 June 1942
		Lt. M.H. Wallace, —	8 June 1942	14 January 1943
		Lt. P.D. Budge, RCN	15 January 1943	19 February 1943
		Lt.Cdr. R.A.S. MacNeil, RCNR	20 February 1943	11 June 1943
		Lt. W.P. Wickett, —	12 June 1943	13 March 1944
		Lt. J.A.M. Levesque, RCNR	14 March 1944	24 January 1945
		Lt. C.W. King, RCNVR	25 January 1945	20 June 1945
STELLARTON	K-457	Lt. R.A. Jarvis, RCNVR	29 September 1944	19 December 1944
		Lt.Cdr. M.G. McCarthy, RCNVR	20 December 1944	26 June 1945
STRATHROY	K-455	Lt.Cdr. W.F. Wood, RCNR	20 November 1944	27 December 1944
		Lt. H.D. Pepper, RCNVR	28 December 1944	31 January 1945
		Lt. J.D. Moore, RCNVR	1 February 1945	6 July 1945
SUDBURY	K-162	Lt.Cdr. A.M. McLarnon, —	15 October 1941	3 May 1943
		Lt. D.S. Martin, —	4 May 1943	27 December 1943
		Lt. G.L. Mackay, RCNR	28 December 1943	19 March 1944
		Lt.Cdr. J.W. Golby, DSC, RCNVR	20 March 1944	28 August 1945
SUMMERSIDE	K-141	Lt.Cdr. F.O. Gerity, —	11 September 1941	21 April 1943
		Lt. G.E. Cross, RCNVR	22 April 1943	31 August 1943
		Lt. G.S. Mongenais, RCNVR	1 September 1943	9 October 1944
		Lt. H.S. Hardy, RCNVR	10 October 1944	17 December 1944
		Lt. F.O. Plant, RCNVR	18 December 1944	2 July 1945
THE PAS	K-168	Lt.Cdr. E.G. Old, —	29 October 1941	14 April 1944
		Lt. R.H. Sylvester, RCNVR	15 April 1944	9 October 1944
		Lt. J.H. Ewart, RCNVR	10 October 1944	19 July 1945
THORLOCK	K-394	Lt. J.E. Francois, RCNR	13 November 1944	10 July 1945
TILLSONBURG	K-496	Lt.Cdr. W. Evans, RCNVR	29 June 1944	26 November 1945
TIMMINS	K-223	Lt. J.A. Brown, —	10 February 1942	30 August 1942
		Lt. J.M. Gillison, —	31 August 1942	11 January 1943
		Lt. N.S.C. Dickinson, —	12 January 1943	19 March 1943
		Lt.Cdr. J.H.S. MacDonald, —	20 March 1943	18 April 1943
		Lt.Cdr. H.S. Maxwell, RCNVR	19 April 1943	1 September 1944

SHIP	'K' NUMBER	COMMANDING OFFICER	FROM	TO
		Lt. R.G. James, RCNVR	2 September 1944	15 December 1944
		Lt. J. Kincaid, RCNR	16 December 1944	10 July 1945
TRAIL	K-174	Lt.Cdr. G.S. Hall, —	30 April 1941	8 October 1943
		Lt. G.M. Hope, RCNVR	9 October 1943	9 October 1944
		Lt. D.J. Lawson, RCNVR	10 October 1944	12 July 1945
TRENTONIAN	K-368	Lt. W.E. Harrison, RCNR	1 December 1943	30 January 1945
		Lt. C.S. Glassco, RCNVR	31 January 1945	22 February 1945
TRILLIUM	K-172	Lt.Cdr. R.F. Harris, —	22 October 1940	14 November 1941
		Lt. H.D. Campsie, —	15 November 1941	8 December 1941
		Skpr.Lt. G.E. Gaudreau, RCNR	9 December 1941	25 February 1942
		Lt. P.E. Evans, RCNR	26 February 1942	21 May 1944
		Lt. K.E. Meredith, RCNVR	22 May 1944	27 June 1945
VANCOUVER	K-240	Lt. P.F.M. DeFreitas, RCNR	20 March 1942	7 June 1943
		Lt.Cdr. A.T. Morrell, RCNR	8 June 1943	4 February 1944
		Lt.Cdr. A.W. Ford, RCNR	5 February 1944	9 October 1944
		Lt. G.C. Campbell, RCNVR	10 October 1944	22 June 1945
VILLE DE QUEBEC	K-242	Lt.Cdr. D.G. Jeffrey, —	24 May 1942	29 September 1942
		Lt. I.H. Bell, —	30 September 1942	11 October 1942
		Lt.Cdr. A.R.E. Coleman, —	12 October 1942	12 June 1943
		Lt. J.L. Carter, RCNVR	13 June 1943	12 March 1944
		Lt. C.S. Glassco, RCNVR	13 March 1944	1 May 1944
		Lt.Cdr. H.C. Hatch, RCNVR	2 May 1944	3 July 1945
WESTYORK	K-369	Lt. M. Smith, RCNR	6 October 1944	29 December 1944
		Lt.Cdr. W.F. Wood, RCNR	30 December 1944	6 July 1945
WETASKIWIN	K-175	Lt.Cdr. G. Windeyer, RCN	17 December 1940	4 November 1942
		Lt. J.R. Kidston, RCNVR	5 November 1942	21 March 1944
		Lt. A. Walton, RCNR	22 March 1944	16 June 1945
WEYBURN	K-173	Lt.Cdr. T.M.W. Golby, RCNR	26 November 1941	22 February 1943
WHITBY	K-346	Lt.Cdr. R.K. Lester, RCNVR	6 June 1944	12 July 1945
WINDFLOWER	K-155	Lt.Cdr. J.H.S. MacDonald, —	4 February 1941	13 October 1941
		Lt. J. Price, —	14 October 1941	7 December 1941
WOODSTOCK	K-238	Lt. L.P. Denny, —	1 May 1942	18 October 1942
		Cdr. G.H. Griffiths, —	19 October 1942	19 January 1943
		Skpr.Lt. J.M. Watson, RCNR	20 January 1943	16 August 1943
		Lt. C.E. Wright, RCNVR	17 August 1943	5 October 1944
		Lt. W. McCombe, RCNR	6 October 1944	18 April 1945
		Lt.Cdr. J.S. Cunningham, RCNVR	19 April 1945	11 March 1946

NOTE

In some cases, where dates were not accurate, the date has been left blank. In others, commanders changed commands on short-term, and often short notice for brief periods, especially in the 1940-42 period and the 1944-45 period. The first was because of the rapid expansion of the ship complement, which allowed Reserve officers chances at command, as the regular officers were released to training establishments. The latter period was when regular officers were given commands to release veteran Reservists for training centers, to pass on their experience.

HMCS BARRIE in the North Atlantic, June 1943. [Public Archives of Canada]

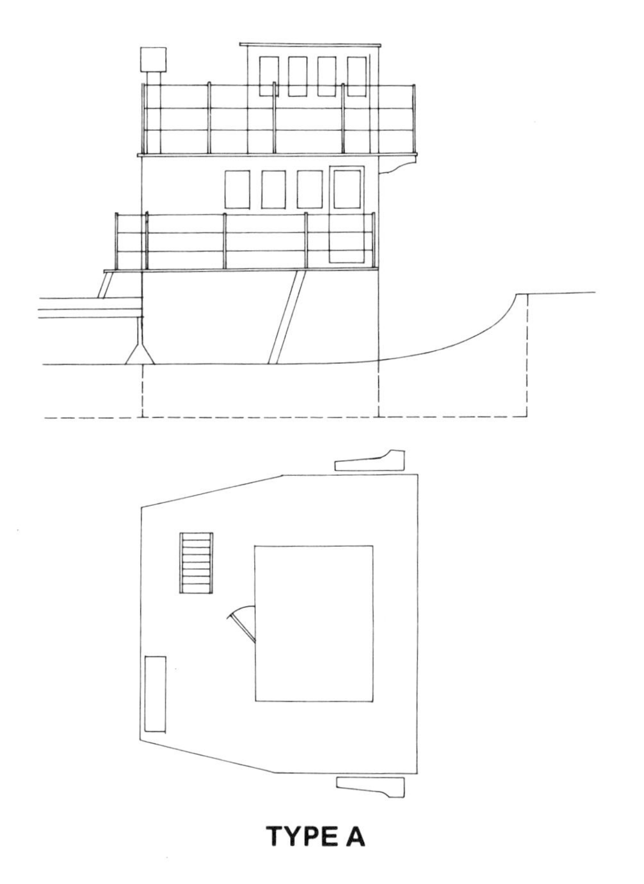

TYPE A

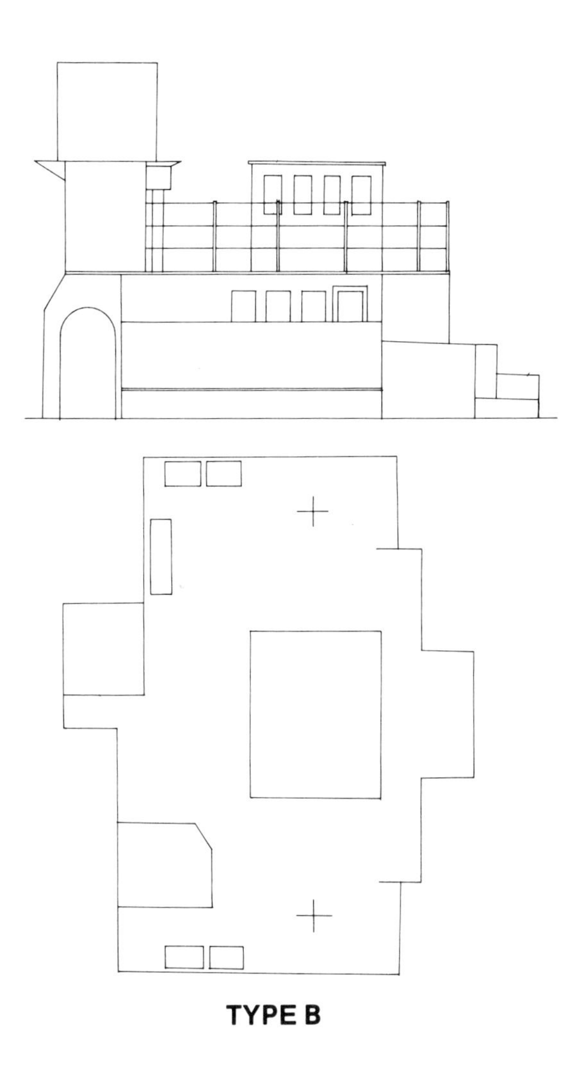

TYPE B

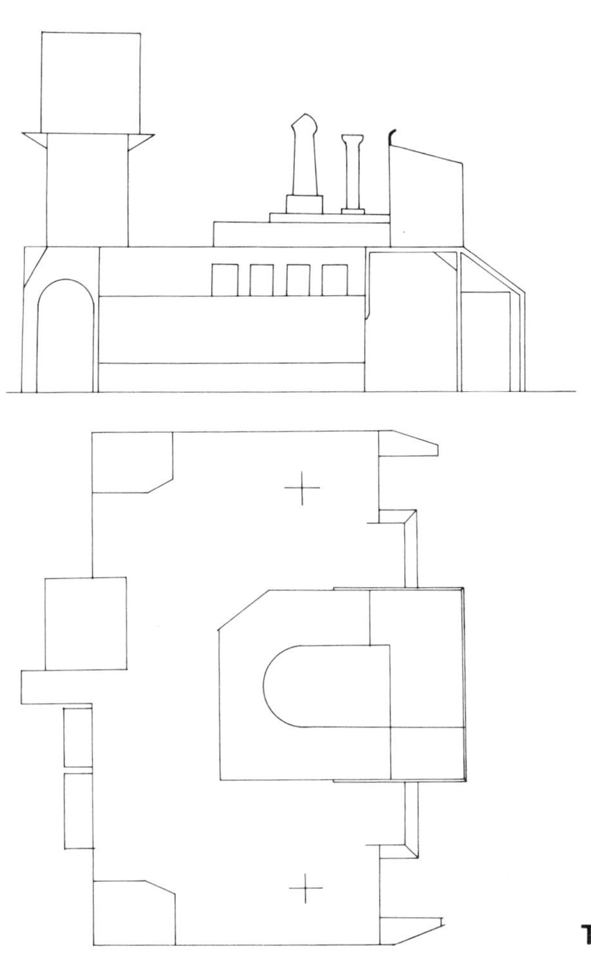

TYPE C

TYPE A
As per Admiralty specifications, this was the first type bridge fitted. Compass house housed all compasses and was intended as a watchkeeper's shelter. Wheel house and chart room were one deck down.

TYPE B
Compass platform widened to accomodate bridge armament and the first 271 radar fitted aft, partially on an extension.

TYPE C
Compass house abolished, compass now open to weather. Asdic compartment fitted to the bridge face. New bracing required to support this structure.

The above were the types fitted with the original flare and sheer of the hull.

By far the most common bridge on all corvettes by 1943, this photo shows a typical layout. The binnacle compass (closest to the viewer) is without its cover. The left door of the overhang is the Asdic hut. The right is to the chart room. The box in the right bridge wing is for the captain, so he can see over the ship's side. The circular tubs are for the 20 mm Oerlikons. Note the teak planks have given away to plywood in the compass deck area only. The semtex over it has worn through. Twin voice pipes on either wing allow conning from either position, to the wheelhouse, one deck below. Others are to the engine room, captain's cabin, wardroom, etc. Binnacle cover can be seen to rear of compass platform. [Maritime Museum of the Atlantic]

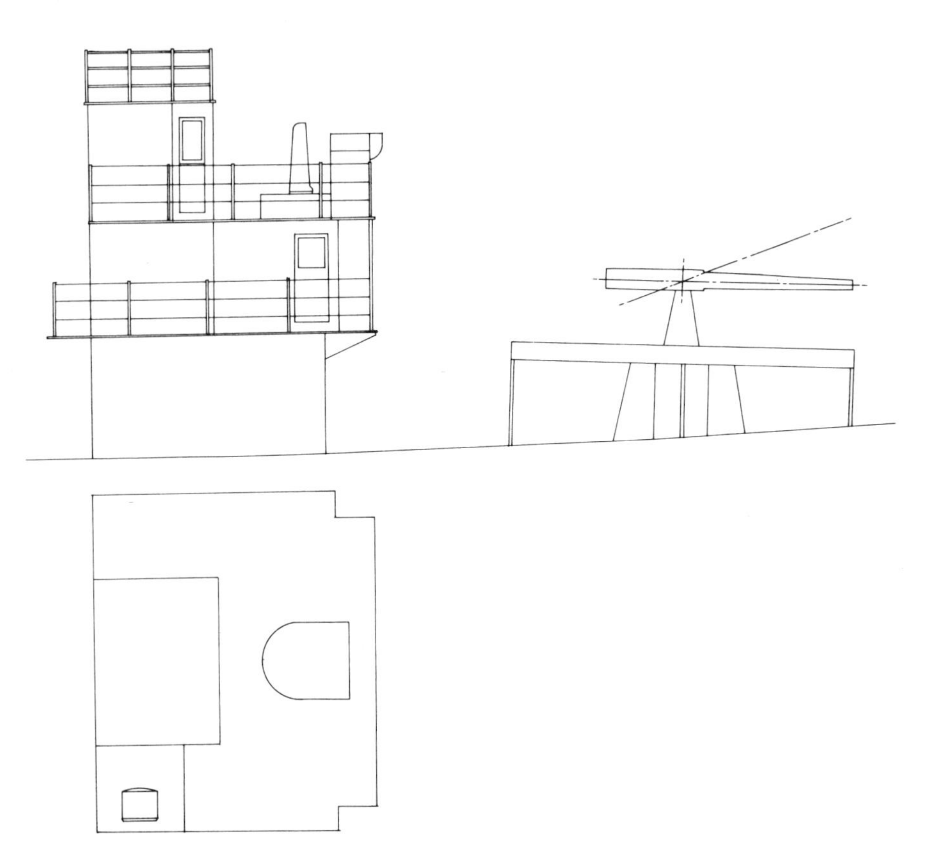

TYPE D
Compass platform heightened by one deck to overlook the 4 inch gun better. Compass house fitted further aft.

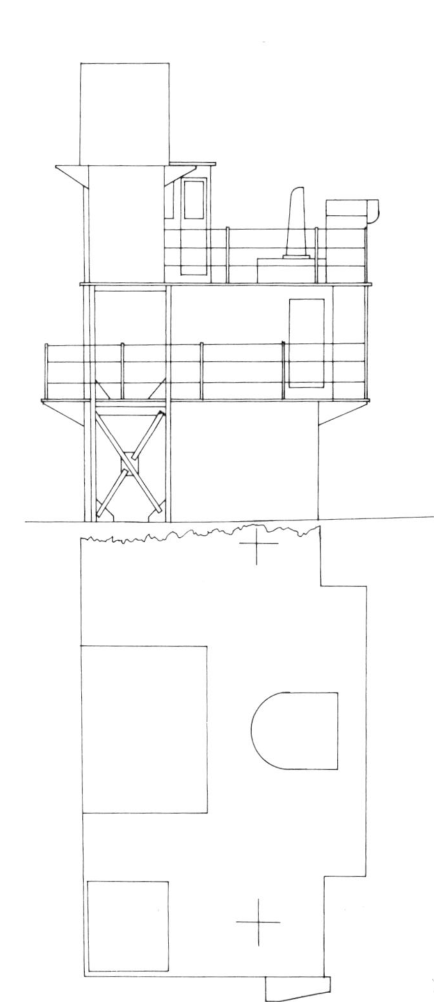

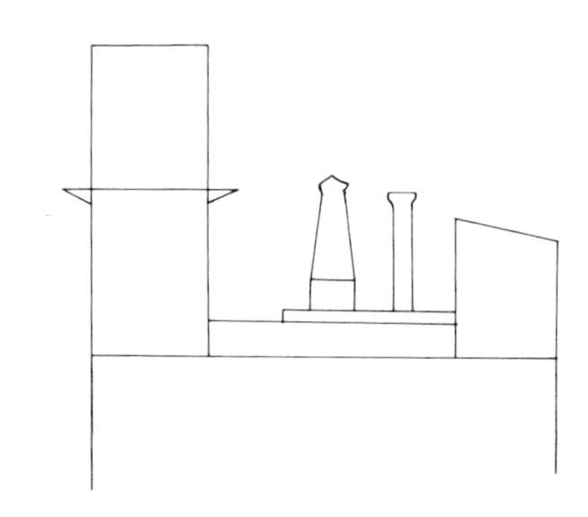

TYPE E
Compass platform widened for accomodation of 20 mm anti-aircraft and 271 radar offset to starboard, in most cases. Diagram shows offset to port, which was the more uncommon.

TYPE F
Compass house abolished, Asdic house moved to overhang the bridge front. Radar still offset in most cases, although some interim corvettes had it centered.

TYPE G
Radar fitted on centerline, on own supports, just abaft the compass platform. This was the final configuration and most corvettes had it by early 1944, although some examples of earlier design hung on until the end of the war. These were very rare though.

Types A through C were the order for Early Flowers. Types D through G were the standard order for Modified Flowers over the latter war years. But no hard and fast rules guide these progressions; rather, corvettes in the interim could possibly see the first bridge of the early Program, and maybe see only the last or second-last.

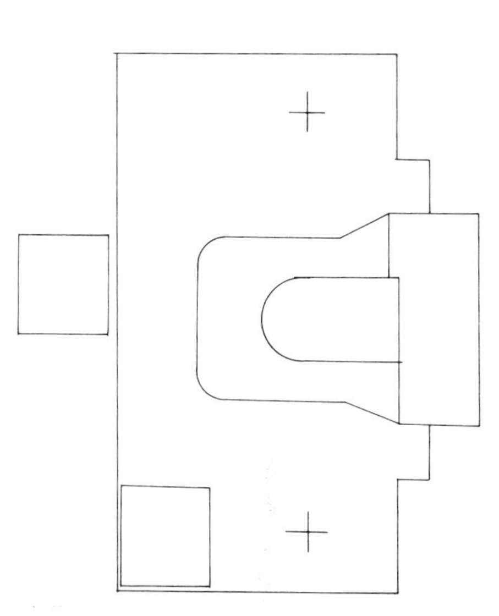

TYPE E

TYPE F

Model of HMCS HALIFAX showing bridge structure, wing extensions to bridge, part of aerial array, foremast, gun and platform. Dodger ahead of foremast provided some protection for storage of flammable stores such as gasoline for pumps and boat's engines. [Author's collection]

FOUR INCH GUN

The 4 inch gun mounted on the corvettes was a World War I model weapon, the first of which was Admiralty supplied. However, with manufacture taken over in Canada by Massey-Harris, the farm tractor people, their model "BL" was the standard mount for the duration. It could be elevated to a limited extent and was never intended for anything other than firing at surfaced U-boats. The ammunition was of the separate shell/propellant type. It was a simple piece, which was very easy to use, after the briefest of training periods.

Drill on a 4 inch gun. Gunner has just opened the breech, allowing fumes to escape. Center rating in white gunshirt is swabbing the bore. This was necessary in this gun because bagged cordite was used with the shell, not a one piece round. Rating to the left is taking cordite from its protective case. Note round holder around circumference of platform with shell in top position and cordite case below. Canvas bucket was used to carry both, to protect shells from nicking and dents from rough handling. Small bell on gunshield signals "cease fire." [Maritime Museum of the Atlantic]

An example of gun shield art on two Massey-Harris BL 4-inch guns. The British BL model was used on only the first few Canadian ships, until Massey-Harris could begin production. Inboard is WETASKIWIN (with her famous wet-ass-queen), outboard is GALT with her skipper paddling the stern sheets of a U-boat. This collection will be published at a later date. [Author's collection via R. A. Broomer]

Behind the gunshield view of a 4 inch BL aboard an undisclosed corvette, June 1941 in Halifax, for the Gunnery School. The simplistic optics for this weapon are apparent. An open grid sight was used for close engagements or rough laying a target, while the reticule telescopic sights were used for finer shooting at longer distances. [Public Archives of Canada via author]

HMCS BRANDON in Halifax Harbor, Nova Scotia, 24 November 1943. BRANDON was one of the odd-balls in the corvette horde, having a matched pair of Hotchkiss 3-pounders on the bridge wings. This was not a temporary fit either. Another view in the author's possession, dated May 1944, shows the other or port Hotchkiss still fitted. No other Canadian corvette had these for this length of time and these were more familiar on early Fairmiles. [Public Archives of Canada via author]

TWO POUNDER POM-POM

Generally, these were of the Vickers-Armstrong type.

A Vickers 2-pounder "pom-pom" anti-aircraft gun (shown here aboard a British minesweeper). [Imperial War Museum]

A Mk. VIII two-pounder pom-pom on a Mk. VIII mount aboard HMCS MORDEN, Halifax, 3 August 1943. An excellent view of this weapon which should help correct the monstrosity that Matchbox includes in their kit! The fire alarm can be seen in the 'tub' as can the two-pdr. shells in the feed bins. Note the Coca Cola cases; what else would one drink with your tot or when sick of coffee? At the far left, the degaussing cables can be seen running down the inside of the bulwarks. Smoke candles can be seen in the corners of the rails atop the boat-house. Note the 'gobs' having a chuckle over this 'staged' shot. [Public Archives of Canada via author]

20 mm OERLIKONS

Usually mounted in two single mounts, one on either wing of the bridge. These were very prized and a waiting list existed for these throughout the war. In 1944, two more were added further aft, but were usually removed when the corvette arrived back in Canadian waters.

A 20 mm Mk. 5 Oerlikon (shown here on HMS HADLEIGH CASTLE, 8 January 1944). [Imperial War Museum]

An alternative used aboard some Canadian corvettes in 1941 was the Hispano 20 mm mount shown here. [Public Archives of Canada]

LEWIS GUNS

The original bridge armament, these were replaced by Browning .303 machine guns. Both were useless for anything, other than anti-aircraft mounts. Replaced by Oerlikons when bridge widened.

Lewis guns of this type were mounted on the wing bridges of corvettes. Here a twin mount with an improvised mount and shield. Full jacketed versions were rare; stripped Lewis's were more common. (Shown here aboard a merchant ship in 1940.) [Author's collection]

MK. VII DEPTH CHARGE

The original requirement of twenty-five depth charges was increased to forty in 1940. These were 300 pound cannister depth bombs, filled with Torpex explosive. They were fired by pressure-sensitive triggers, which were pre-set in the final moments before being dropped over the fantail or being fired by the depth charge thrower. They were usually dropped and fired in patterns of ten, which resulted in, roughly, a diamond pattern. They were lethal within twenty feet of the U-boat's hull.

Loading a Mark VII depth charge aboard HMCS AGASSIZ, February 1944. This shows the screw-out detonator (center); the other two plugs are where Torpex could be removed or added at disposal or at the manufacturer's. [Public Archives of Canada]

An inert 300 pound depth charge, displayed at Maritime Museum, Halifax, Nova Scotia. The man's hand gives some idea of size. The man, a veteran, was a bo'sun aboard corvettes and frigates during the war. [Author's collection]

The end plate in a Mark VII. The hydrostatic pistol is missing (center) and the Torpex removed through the two circular access plates. Note it was dismantled at Bedford Magazine, September 1968. [Author's collection]

One of the reasons that minesweeping davits were still aboard Canadian corvettes in latter stages of the Atlantic war is apparent in this shot. This is HMCS AGASSIZ in 1942, with the small racks still fitted. However, the powered davits were superior to the block and tackle rigs later fitted. [via author]

HMCS PORT ARTHUR—a typical quarterdeck and fantail while painting goes on. Note the smoke candle position, the spare cordage, the anti-icing covers and the later-style degaussing coil. Note the ashcan with the "ashcans." This configuration of racks was common on the Modified Flowers and later corvettes. [via author]

HMCS SOREL on 10 April 1944 in Halifax. For those of you wondering what should appear on the spartan afterdeck of the Matchbox kit, this should give you some idea. Note the anti-ice covers over the doubled depth charge racks to prevent the depth charges from freezing in the racks. Note the trap control levers at the very stern. [via author]

A photo of ex-LOUISBURG's stern, showing the depth charge rails and traps in the stern rail. [Maritime Museum of the Atlantic]

HEDGEHOG

In late 1942, a new weapon against the U-boat was introduced. This was a multiple spigot mortar-type weapon, firing twenty-four rounds, filled with 36 pounds of Torpex, with each bomb weighing 65 pounds. These were fired sequentially, 230 yards in front of the ship and formed an elliptical pattern, while the vessel still had Asdic contact. Eight full patterns were stored aboard (192). They were not fused until in water, and were therefore contact fused, meaning they did not explode until they hit something. Thus a U-boat kill was assured if they exploded. These eventually evolved into the "Squid" multiple mortar, but were not mounted on corvettes, being too heavy. What was fitted was a special "Split Hedgehog," with two mounts of twelve either side of the 4 inch mount. However, these lacked the reassuring 'crump' of the depth charge and the attendant 'shaking-up' of the U-boat crew, so they never really replaced the depth charge.

Hedgehog aboard HMCS MOOSE JAW, early 1943. The detonator caps are still in place, atop the mortar rounds. [Public Archives of Canada]

The rear side of a Hedgehog mortar, as the operator saw it. The hand wheel controlled offset angle to either side and the control at the top right controlled the pitch fore and aft. The Stabilizer Receiver, Type "Q," Mk. II, was a later addition which automatically stabilized the mortar bed against ship roll and pitch, but was limited by the limits of movement in the table itself. A gyro unit below decks acted through this unit. Control box to the left (with protective bars) shows arc of elevation to left, degrees of offset to right. Box to right, top, has adjustable range input crank. Firing button peers over the hand wheel. [Public Archives of Canada via author]

The Hedgehog as mounted on a minesweeper, probably an Algerine. Taken on 12 July 1943, this photograph shows the spigots of the mortar proper, with the firing pins centered in each spigot. As can be seen, the rows of spigots could be angled to port or starboard. Fore and aft changes in angle were accomplished by rocking the entire table on a gymbal. [Public Archives of Canada via author]

HMCS NORTH BAY, October 1943. A staged photograph, showing the drill for reloading the Hedgehog spigot antisubmarine mortar. This was the first positive improvement over the World War I depth charge and although deadly when used accurately, was never as popular as the depth charge. The bombs are all Mk. I and II's, weighing 65 pounds as marked. Both would be equipped with the Primer No. 13 Mk. II BR in the fuse hole atop the warhead if being used in earnest. The yellow warhead bands denote practice bombs. [Public Archives of Canada via author]

Ships of the Royal Canadian Navy followed the examples set by the Royal Navy pretty well throughout the war years. Only after the war was over did the RCN start to deviate from accepted Admiralty colors. However, let us begin in the pre-war years.

During the late 1930's, Canadian ships used a dark gray (AP 503A) and light gray (AP 503C) [AP = Admiralty Pattern]. Most destroyers of the RCN during this time can be seen sporting light gray overall. But with the outbreak of war, new colors or shades were introduced: dark gray; light gray; a 50-50 mixture of the former and white; and white. To these were added two shades of blue, B5 and B6. However, Canadian bo'suns, remembering how their mothers added 'bluing' to the water to make whites whiter, added B5 to the white to make it whiter! Proportions added varied, but the average appears to be about less than a quarter pint per five gallon pail.

In late 1940/early 1941, these were superceeded by the MS series of colors, but the older paints lingered on until paint stores were used up. Thus both types overlapped and hard and fast identification of photos is not possible at all times, in respect to time periods. The MS series started with MS1, gray-black, and lightened towards MS 4A, mid-gray.

Meanwhile, the noted naturalist Sir Peter Scott had evolved his novel camouflage pattern, utilizing pastel shades of green, blue, and white. Admiralty officers were horrified to think of large areas of His Majesty's Ships being painted white, but trials were carried out and under subdued lighting conditions it was found that the paint scheme significantly reduced or distorted the ships' silhouette.

Western Approaches schemes, as they became known when the Admiralty accepted them, changed throughout the years 1941-1944, with B20 being substituted for WA blue during 1941-1942 on; some Canadian ships. HMCS *Sackville* is a good example. Standard patterns involved painting the ship off-white or pale green overall, and painting various panels of WA blue and green on the hull and/or superstructure. The pale green overall was a Canadian variant and B20 was substituted for the WA green or a medium green was used. However, these were fairly rare.

It must be stressed that these were matt finish paints, and the WA paint scheme was only effective if the paint was kept free of rust or dirt stains. Since the escort vessels of 1942-1943 were so overworked, it was very unusual to see a prime example of this scheme, unless the vessel was newly out of drydock. Also, an added factor was the very nature of the paint. Color varied with surface preparation, what was used to dilute the paint, if the paint had been frozen and, most of all, what the state of mind was of the matlot who applied it! If he was hung-over and painting from a bo'sun's chair in near-freezing temperatures, over salt-caked plates or was anticipating the 1100 hours rum tot, it can be imagined what sort of job was done.

By 1943 these colors had been largely standardized and a comprehensive new line of colors introduced, each having a code letter followed by a number, which denoted its reflective value as compared to white, which was set at 100%. These were termed "G" and "B" series. Hence G5 Gray had a reflective value of 5% and appeared near-black, unless compared to black, where the difference was apparent. "G" series usually denoted gray-based colors and "B" blue-based, but there were exceptions such as G20, which contained green pigment and hence was a greenish-gray hue. But as the war continued, G20 was replaced by B20 because of shortages in raw materials. It should be noted that both colors had a reflective value of 20% of that of white. About this same time WA green was slowly replaced by B55, which was the same as WA blue.

HMCS LA PAS at Digby, Nova Scotia, in 1944. Overall medium gray hull, light gray upperworks. [Maritime Museum of the Atlantic, McBride collection]

Of interest to the corvette enthusiast would be the experiments that were carried out aboard HMCS *Rimouski* and *Edmunston* in early 1945. At dusk and in dim moonlight, ships could be seen as dark silhouettes. What was done was to *light* the hulls and upperworks with a diffused glow, matching the light of the night horizon in intensity, which was controlled by photoelectric cells. The two ships, in a series of tests, approached to within 300 yards of the target before being seen, when the target had been visible at 650 yards! Of course at this date very little use would have been gained, as radar was becoming standard on almost anything that could float, but it was felt that it would help confuse lookouts if they could not see what the radar could, even at close ranges.[3]

However, for the period late 1944 to 1945, a radical camouflage change came about. Ships were needed less and less in European waters and British build-ups in the Pacific were imminent. Canada went along with this, as she would have ships in the Pacific,

HMCS CHICOUTIMI, in 1943-1944, leaving Digby harbor. Medium gray lower hull, light gray upperworks and hull. Note how the rust and dirt does not materially affect the scheme's effect. [Maritime Museum of the Atlantic, McBride collection]

3. RCN press release 1648, 20 February 1946.

too. The WA scheme had proven well in the North Atlantic, but now more coastal work would be necessary and with it camouflage that would prove effective at shorter range. Accordingly, AFO 2106/43 was issued, in which gloss or half-gloss paint superceded the matt finishes of before. Where in most cases the camouflage patterns had varied from one side of a ship from the other, this would not be the case in future. The hull was to be painted G55 or G45 overall. Decks and horizontal surfaces were to be painted B30 or G20, if visible from outboard.[4] Semtex surfaces were no longer to be painted. The mast, crow's nest, all small fittings, the underside of blast shields, flag decks, gun platforms, sponsons, plus the tops of any surface which would reflect light into dark areas were to be painted white.[5] The same with the bottoms of boats and gun barrels. The false silhouette shown in the drawing was to be painted with B20 or G45, but the greater number were painted the former. The size of panel was stated in Naval Orders 3873, Paragraph 10, and were to be within two feet of correct measurement. This was not always done however, and exaggerated panels were common. Full specifications for the above were issued to the RCN on 15 October 1944.

An alternative to the above, and indeed throughout the war were the Admiralty Disruptive patterns. On RN ships these were standardized somewhat, but on Canadian ships, the bo'sun, often working from poor illustrations, let his and the men's imaginations have a free hand. Hence, the colors used were whatever was aboard at the time orders were received. For some strange reason, shore facilities were loath to supply adequate supplies of paint to RCN ships and what was supplied was of vastly inferior quality to what was issued to RN ships. Hence, a practice of painting ship in U.K. ports

4. CB 3098 (R), paragraph 143, 144.
5. CB 3098 (R), paragraph 74.

HMCS BRANTFORD, 1944, off Digby CNR wharf. Note the modified Western Approaches scheme of three colors: light gray, medium gray on the band, dark green ahead, and off-white to foreshorten the hull. This was quite common. Off-white on the upperworks. [Maritime Museum of the Atlantic, McBride collection]

became commonplace, the paint drawn from HM Stores, after 'deep sixing' the Canadian goods. Common sense is the modeler's only guide to doing a Disruptive pattern.

Painting a Scale Model

This portion of this appendix is intended entirely for the scale modeler and the illustrator. Consideration was given to color plates and/or chips, but because of variants such as the printer not being able to certify color fidelity or in the case of paint chips, variants such as humidity, air pressure, temperature, and exposure to light, it was decided that a chart, showing how to mix these colors would be most appropriate.

However, even this was not easy. The only work ever done on this facet of ships of the Second World War is out of print and personally the author was unable to obtain one. However, through a friend in the Maritime Museum of the Atlantic, ways were found. Actual comparison with Canadian "G" and "B" color chips was made possible. An article, dated 15 years ago, gave broad hints as to color mixes, but using no longer available brands. Experimentation—trial and error—proved to be the only real recourse.

Accordingly, the accompanying chart was prepared and using our trial and error method, plus comparison, these colors appeared. All use Humbrol colors and numbers and are based on Humbrol white No. 34 matt finish, unless otherwise stated. Measurement of added colors was via a No. 1 watercolor brush and the paints used *must* be thoroughly mixed, so they will drip in uniform drops. Eye droppers were tried, but the size of the drops varied with pressure. Humbrol does not fill its tins, which is a God-send. *Do not* try using other brands with this chart, unless you want to experiment!

Special Effects for Models

If using the Peter Scott scheme or Western Approaches, effective weathering is a must for realism. This paint was only 'fresh' just after re-fit or after painting. Long days at sea caused scouring of the paint, lifting sections often as large as a dinner plate from the original base coat underneath. Rust from upper deck fittings and anchor, and, to a lesser extent, carbon from the funnel, discolored the paintwork. Brushes with pilings, bumpers, etc., blackened or further removed paint. A suitable rust paint is available from shops that cater to the armor buff and is suitable for this application also. You may make your own, but remember to keep it a light red-orange for scale effect. It should streak from drains, hawse holes, plate edges, and any other opening in the bulwarks or superstructure. These ships endured savage treatment both from action and the stormy North Atlantic.

Rigging, such as aerials, should sag somewhat, as should the wire rails. The ones the author has seen on the Matchbox kit should be discarded, saving only the stanchions. Canvas shrouds, made from tissue and painted Humbrol No. 72, should be

HMCS COLLINGWOOD, at Digby, in late 1944-early 1945. A Disruptive pattern which was common in the latter part of the war was the overall pale gray, with the medium gray false hull. [Maritime Museum of the Atlantic, McBride collection]

COLOR CHART

	Color	Usage	Pre-War	1940-41	1941-42	1943-44	1945-46	Drops of mix paint to add to tin of matte white	Remarks
1	Gray-black				MS1	G5		None	Humbrol #77
2	Very dark gray	AP	507A	507A	507A & M52	G10		None	Humbrol #27
3	Dark gray			50%	50%				50-50 mixture, line #2 and #9
4	Dark blue-gray				B5	B15	B15	None	Humbrol #79
5	Mid green-gray	Camouflage			MS3	G20		110/30	30 being color to add
6	Mid blue					B20	B20	130/25	25 being added color
7	Mid gray				MS4			50/33	33 being added color
8	Mid blue-gray				B6	B30		30/25	25 being added color
9	Light gray	AP	507C	507C	507C & MS4A	G45	G45	10/33	33 being added color
10	Pale blue			WA blue		B55	B55	15/25	WA = Western Approaches
11						G55			1 part G20 to 4 parts white
12	Pale green			WA green				None	Humbrol #90; North Atlantic only
13	Teak deck							20/29	29 being color added
14	Semtex							50/33	33 added color; deck overlay
15	Deck gray							None	Humbrol #88
16	Hull red							None	Humbrol #70; anti-foul 'lead'
17	Black							None	Humbrol #33; funnel tops, etc.
18	White							None	Humbrol #34; base coat of WA and Peter Scott schemes

secured by thread and placed on the Oerlikons, pom-pom, and hedgehog—especially when shown in port or during severe weather—depending on the modeler. A tompion was fitted to the 4 inch main armament when not on active duty or during action station situations.

If modeling a 1942 or 1943 corvette, the illumination rocket rails were seldom fitted to the 4 inch. Later, in 1944, these were fitted, especially in the RCN.

The green Maple Leaf became a standard item on the funnel of all Canadian ships in 1944, under Naval Spec. 3960, but many ships wore them long before. Some early examples had as many as three in a cluster.

Carley floats were only standardized in color in 1944; use Humbrol No. 99. Previously they had been keyed to the surrounding camouflage pattern.

For added realism, dents can be added to the ship's stem, sides, and stern. Corvette "drivers," as the RCNVR captains liked to refer to themselves, were inexperienced—some until wars' end.

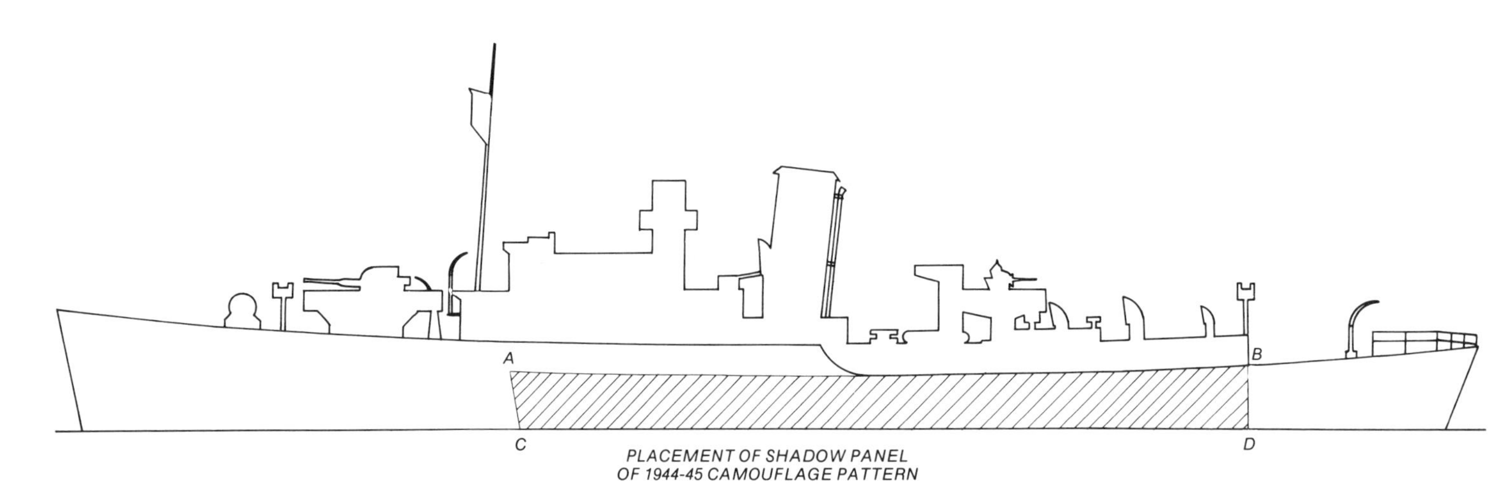

PLACEMENT OF SHADOW PANEL
OF 1944-45 CAMOUFLAGE PATTERN

AC is parallel with the stem.

BD is vertical.

AB is the line of the upper deck or top of bulwarks where these exist.

A is abreast of the face of the bridge.

B is abreast of the after end of the superstructure.

Drawn by Ray Merriam from copy of Naval Order 3873 (15 October 1944 — but in effect since early summer with some RCN units, especially destroyers) supplied by author.

In 1945 and early 1946, Crown Assets Disposal Corporation, having taken delivery of nearly all the corvettes as well as other warships no longer wanted or needed, began to sell off these surplus vessels. Some of the older corvettes, although only two or three years old, were completely worn out, their tasks had been so hard and continuous, and so they were scrapped.

Quite a few, however, were sold to Central and South American interests. Others went to Greek, Canadian, and Mid-Eastern interests where they were turned into merchant or passenger/freight vessels.

The author, in researching this segment of the corvette story, was saddened to think that at least one example of this class of escort vessel had not been saved for future generations. However, there is one in Canadian hands; formerly the corvette *Sackville* which had been used by various government departments, such as Department of Transport, Marine Division, and currently by the Canadian Oceanographic Institute in Dartmouth, Nova Scotia. Since the early 1970's, *Sackville* was in semi-retirement, but has since been reinstated as a fully functioning vessel because of a tight money situation not allowing for anticipated ship acquisitions. With the loss of the two Dominican corvettes, ex-*Lachute* and ex-*Louisburg II* to Hurricane "David," 31 August 1979, *Sackville* is the last surviving hope that Maritime Museum of the Atlantic has for a restorable corvette. Speaking to a Museum representative, it was disclosed that *Sackville* will have to remain on active service for another 5-7 years until money restraints are eased. After being informed by

Ex-PETROLIA, now MAID OF ATHENS, in Halifax Harbor, 1946. She later became BHARATLAXMI, registered to Bharat Line. She was last registered with Lloyd's in 1964, when she was refused registry. [McBride collection, Maritime Museum of the Atlantic]

BEDFORD II (ex-GALLOWAY KENT, ex-HMCS NORTH BAY). She operated in North American coastal waters until the early 1960's. [McBride collection, Maritime Museum of the Atlantic]

NORTH SHORE, ex-HMCS LINDSAY. Converted by Clare Shipyards, Meteghan, Nova Scotia, for Clarke Steamship, Montreal, Quebec. Served the north shore of the St. Lawrence and the Gulf as an express passenger/freighter from 1946 to 1961, when she was sold to Typaldos Brothers of Greece; re-named LIMNOS. Original conversion cost $300,000. [Clarke Transport]

Photo taken in the spring of 1979 of two Dominican Republic corvettes, #401 COLON (ex-HMCS LA CHUTE) and #402 JUAN ALEJANDRO (ex-LOUISBURG II) at Las Calderas Naval Base. Canada was attempting to buy back LOUISBURG for restoration as a museum piece. It would have resided in Halifax, Nova Scotia, at the Maritime Museum of the Atlantic. Both corvettes were driven ashore in a severe hurricane in August 1979 and battered beyond repair. Parts will be used to repair SACKVILLE which has remained in Canadian hands since she was laid down. [Maritime Museum of the Atlantic]

DND sources in 1980 that *Sackville* would have to soldier on for at least five to seven years, it was feared that the ship would not be restorable when finally released. While taping a session for a local television programme on the *Sackville*, it was learned that the ship's yearly refit had been cancelled in January 1982. Digging deeper, it was disclosed that *Sackville* would be declared surplus in the Spring of 1982 and with proper warning to Museum staff and veterans' associations, it is a near-sure thing that *Sackville* will retire to become a museum exhibit at the Maritime Museum of the Atlantic, Halifax, N.S. However funding for restoration has not yet been forthcoming.

What remains of the two Dominican corvettes ex-LACHUTE (401) and ex-LOUISBURG II (402). Hit by Hurricane David at Las Calderas Naval Base, Dominican Republic on 31 August 1979, both ships were damaged beyond repair. Both will be scrapped at that location. [G.F. Smith Marine Systems]

Where did they go? Here are a few examples the author was able to trace. In some cases the accompanying photos speak for themselves.

Chile: *Stellerton* (K-457), *Strathroy* (K-455), *Thorlock* (K-394).

Venezuela: *Amherst* (K-148), *Dunvegan* (K-177), *Oakville* (K-178), *Battleford* (K-165), *Kamsack* (K-171)—lost on Chebucto Head in transit, and *Wetaskiwin* (K-175). One other lost during transit.

Greece: *Petrolia* (K-498)—converted to freighter *Maid of Athens*. See photo.

Canada: *North Bay* (K-399)—converted to merchantman *Bedford II*, *Lindsay* (K-338)—converted to fast passenger/frieght ship *North Shore*, *St. Thomas* (K-488) converted to coastal merchantman *Camosun*, 1946, *Chilcotin*, 1957, *Yukon Star*, 1958.

Dominican Republic: *LaChute* (K-440), *Louisburg* (K-401), *Peterborough* (K-342), *Belleville* (K-332), *Riviere du Loup* (K-357), and *Asbestos* (K-358). Refitted in St. John, New Brunswick, in 1947 for the trip south. *Asbestos* was lost in transit. *LaChute* and *Louisburg II* were only current survivors.

K-15 *Atholl*, scrapped Canada, October 1952.

K-104 *Dawson*, foundered at Hamilton, Ontario, 22 March 1946.

K-141 *Summerside*, scrapped Canada June 1946.

K-172 *Trillium*, RCN 1941-1945, mercantile *Olympic Runner*, 1950, *Otori Maru No. 10*, 1956.

K-173 *Woodstock*, mercantile *Olympic Winner*, 1951, *Otori Maru No. 20*, 1956, *Akitsu Maru*, 1957.

K-174 *Trail*, scrapped Canada, August 1950.

K-223 *The Pas*, mercantile *Guayaquil* (ex-*Trujillo*, 1948), lost 3 August 1950.

K-225 *Kitchener*, scrapped Canada, September 1949.

K-275 *Giffard* (ex-HMS *Budleia*), RCN 1944, scrapped Canada, October 1952.

K-333 *Cobourg*, mercantile *Cameo* 1945, *Dundas Kent*, 1948, *Puerto del Sol*, 1951.

K-335 *Frontenac*, disposed, 1946.

K-340 *Owen Sound*, mercantile *Cadio*, 1946.

K-341 *Parry Sound*, mercantile *Olympic Champion*, 1950, *Otori Maru No. 15*, 1956.

K-343 *St. Lambert*, mercantile *Chrysi Hondroulis*, 1946, *Loula*, 1955.

K-345 *Smith Falls*, mercantile *Olympic Lightning*, 1950, *Otori Maru No. 16*, 1956.

K-346 *Whitby*, disposed of 30 August 1946.

K-358 *Asbestos*, scrapped New Orleans, March 1949.

K-369 *West York*, mercantile *Guatemala*, 1946, *Moulay Bouchaib*, 1946, *Espresso*, 1953, *Federal Express*, 1960, lost 5 May 1960.

K-415 *Hawksbury*, mercantile *Campuhea*, 1950, scrapped Hong Kong, 1956.

K-520 *Norsyd*, mercantile *Balboa*, 1948, Israeli *Haganah*, 1950, scrapped, 1956.

K-540 *Beauharnois*, Israeli *Wedgewood*, 1950, scrapped 1956.

Canadian Forces Auxiliary Vessel (CFAV) SACKVILLE, formerly the corvette of the same name during World War II (K-181). Time has come full circle in this photo: SACKVILLE, built in December 1941, often tied up here at Jetty 5, formerly known as "Corvette Jetty" during the war. Thirty-eight years later, she returns to Jetty 5 as the only surviving Canadian corvette, although now heavily altered. Taken 28 November 1979, she is the last hope for a restored ship of this, Canada's largest escort class. [Canadian Armed Forces]

K-686 *Fergus*, mercantile *Camco II*, 1945, *Harcourt Kent*, 1948, lost 22 November 1949.

K-687 *Guelph*, mercantile *Guelph*, 1946, *Josephine Lanasa*, 1955, *Burfin*, 1956.

K-688 *Merritonia*, lost off the coast of Nova Scotia, 30 November 1945.

ADDENDUM

On the night of 21 November 1943, a fast convoy bound from Gibraltar for the United Kingdom was joined by the corvettes *Calgary* and *Snowberry*, the frigate *Nene*, and the anti-aircraft cruiser *Prince Robert*. The convoy had been attacked by glider bombs and aircraft earlier that day, but now the escorts would grapple with an older known enemy, the U-boat.

Nene gained a radar contact while the convoy was some five hundred miles west of Cape Finisterre, which proved to be a surfaced U-boat. *Nene* and *Calgary* set off in pursuit and after a hot chase, the U-boat was exposed by starshell from *Calgary*. The U-boat was engaged at 3,700 yards and a hit was noted on the U-boat's casing, followed by the latter firing a torpedo and then diving. *Nene* avoided the torpedo and the hunt was on.

Calgary and *Nene* depth-charged the area, time and again, for over an hour without result. *Snowberry* joined, and establishing a good contact, laid a full pattern of depth charges over the area. An underwater explosion was noted, and *Nene*, now in contact, made a final run with 20 depth charges. Out of the resultant upheaval, the tower of the U-boat emerged, on *Snowberry*'s starboard bow, bobbing up and down in the heaving waters.

Slowly the U-boat gathered way, while the three ships pounded her with everything that would bear. The German crew were swept from the decks as they emerged and the tower holed time and again by hits from the pom-poms and 4 inch shells. Slowly she lost way and began to settle by the stern, while the panic-stricken Germans could be seen leaping for their lives. Fire was checked while the crew abandoned and within moments the U-boat disappeared in a welter of spray, oil and flotsam. *Snowberry* and *Calgary* retrieved the oil-covered survivors.

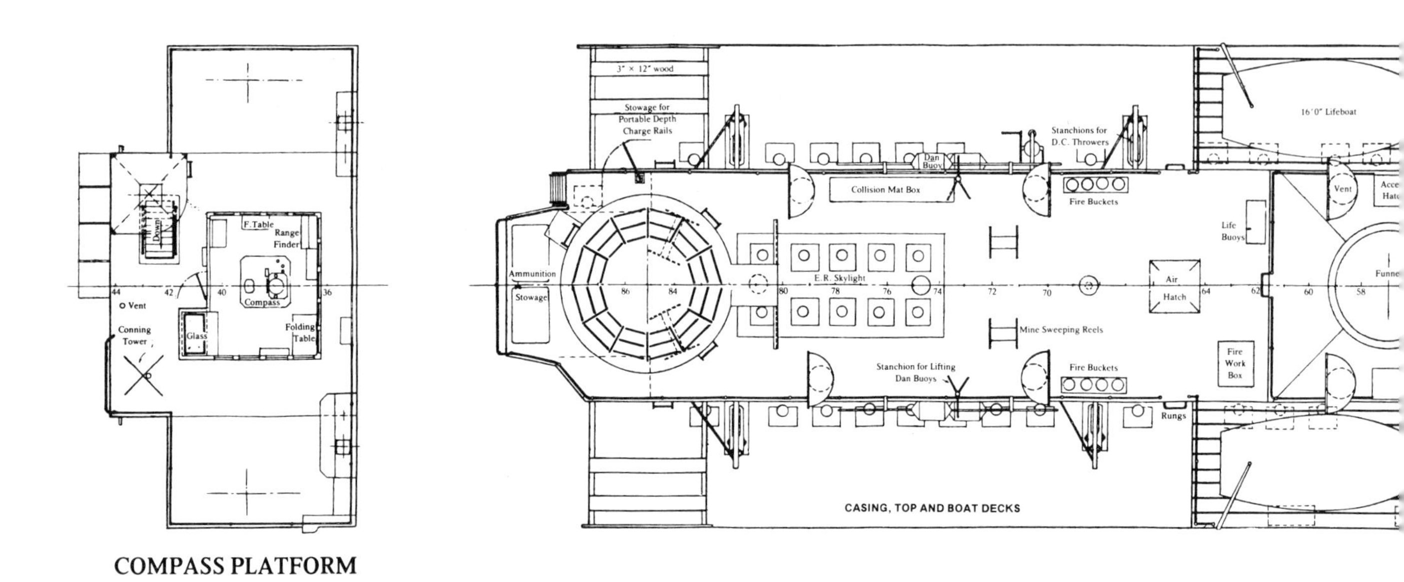

F.Table
Range Finder
Down
Vent
Conning Tower
Glass
Compass
Folding Table
COMPASS PLATFORM
3" × 12" wood
Stowage for Portable Depth Charge Rails
Dan Buoy
Stanchions for D.C. Throwers
16'0" Lifeboat
Collision Mat Box
Fire Buckets
Vent
Life Buoys
Ammunition
Stowage
E.R. Skylight
Air Hatch
Funnel
Mine Sweeping Reels
Stanchion for Lifting Dan Buoys
Fire Buckets
Fire Work Box
Rungs
CASING, TOP AND BOAT DECKS

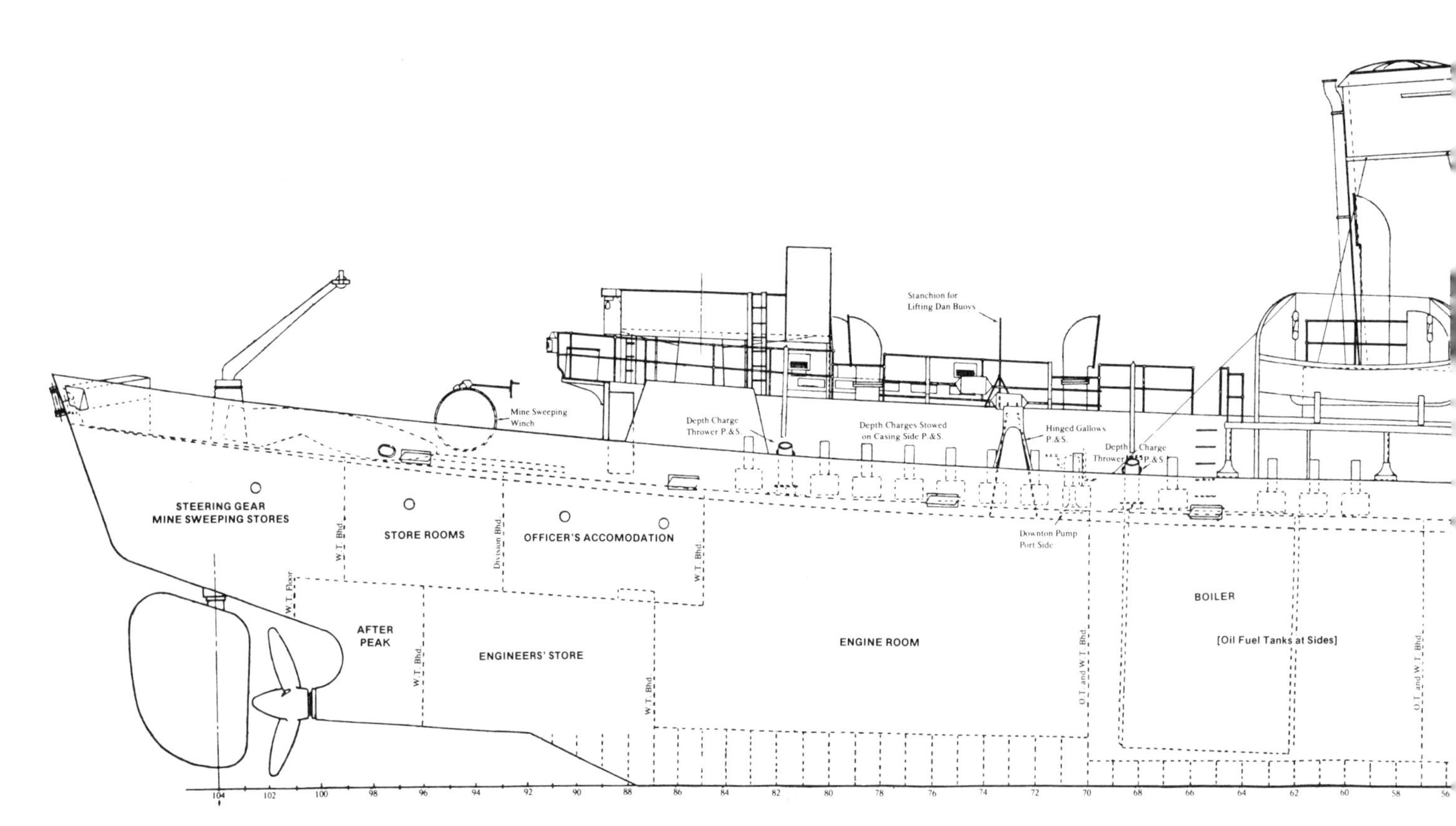

Stanchion for Lifting Dan Buoys
Mine Sweeping Winch
Depth Charge Thrower P.&S.
Depth Charges Stowed on Casing Side P.&S.
Hinged Gallows P.&S.
Depth Charge Thrower P.&S.
STEERING GEAR MINE SWEEPING STORES
W.T. Bhd.
STORE ROOMS
Division Bhd.
OFFICER'S ACCOMODATION
W.T. Bhd.
Downton Pump Port Side
W.T. Floor
AFTER PEAK
W.T. Bhd.
ENGINEERS' STORE
W.T. Bhd.
ENGINE ROOM
O.T. and W.T. Bhd.
BOILER
[Oil Fuel Tanks at Sides]
O.T. and W.T. Bhd.

PROFILE AND DECK PLANS
H.M.C.S. EDMUNDSTON (P.V. 64)
Yarrows Ltd., Esquimalt, B.C.
23 August 1941

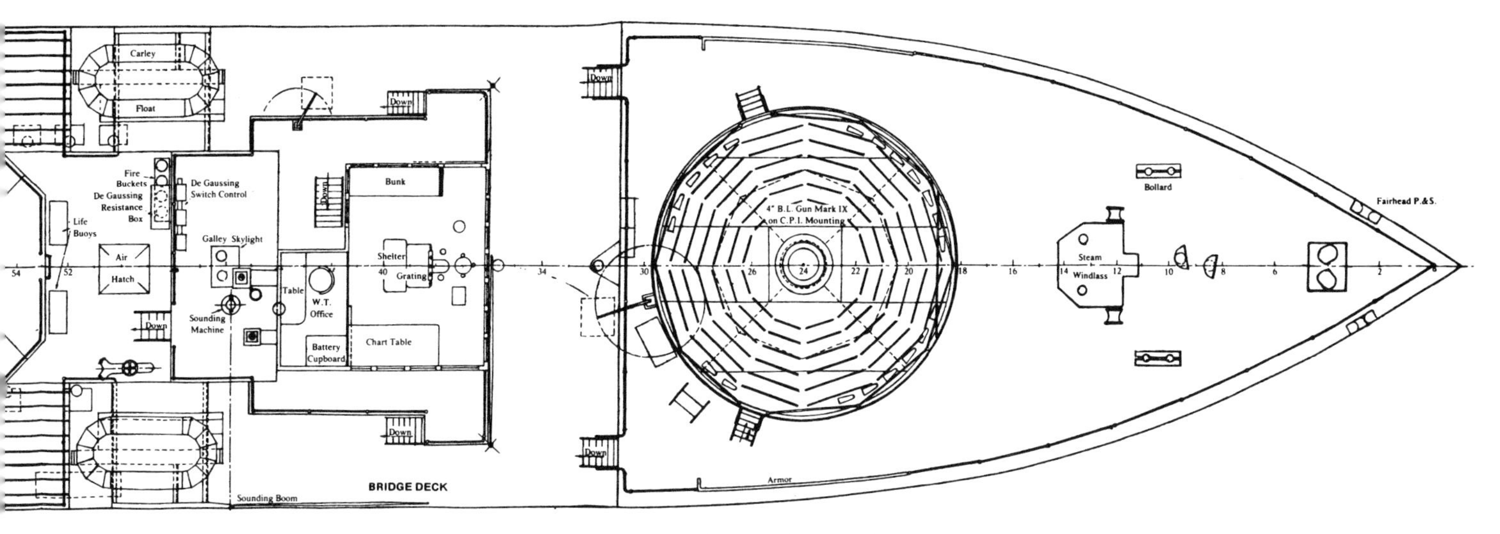

FORECASTLE DECK

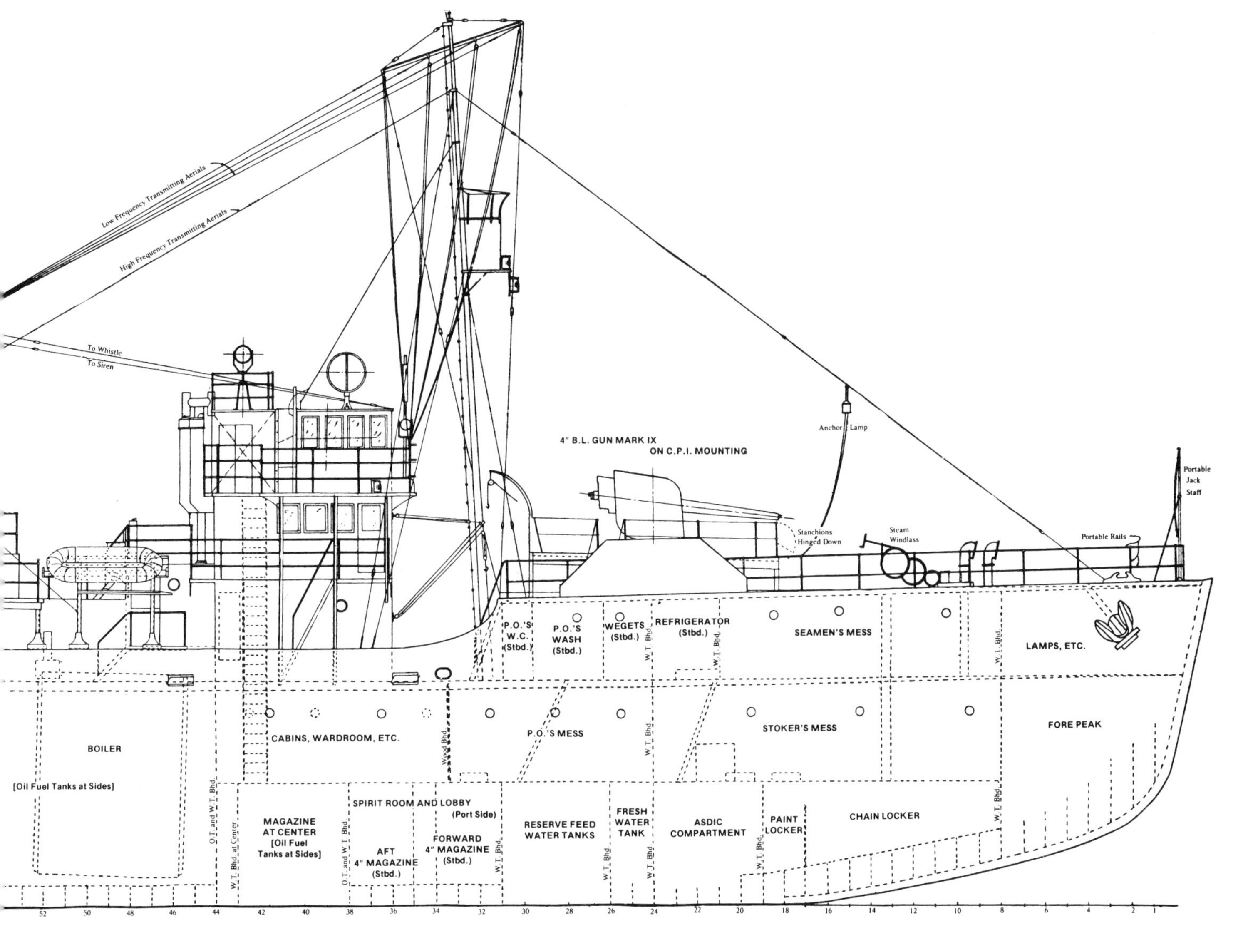

ILE

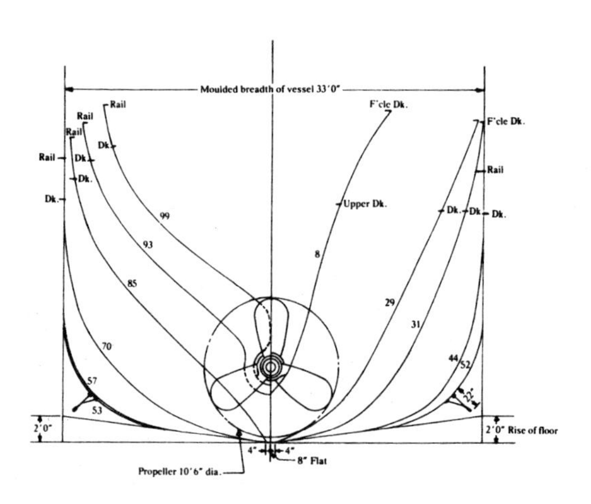

BODY SECTIONS

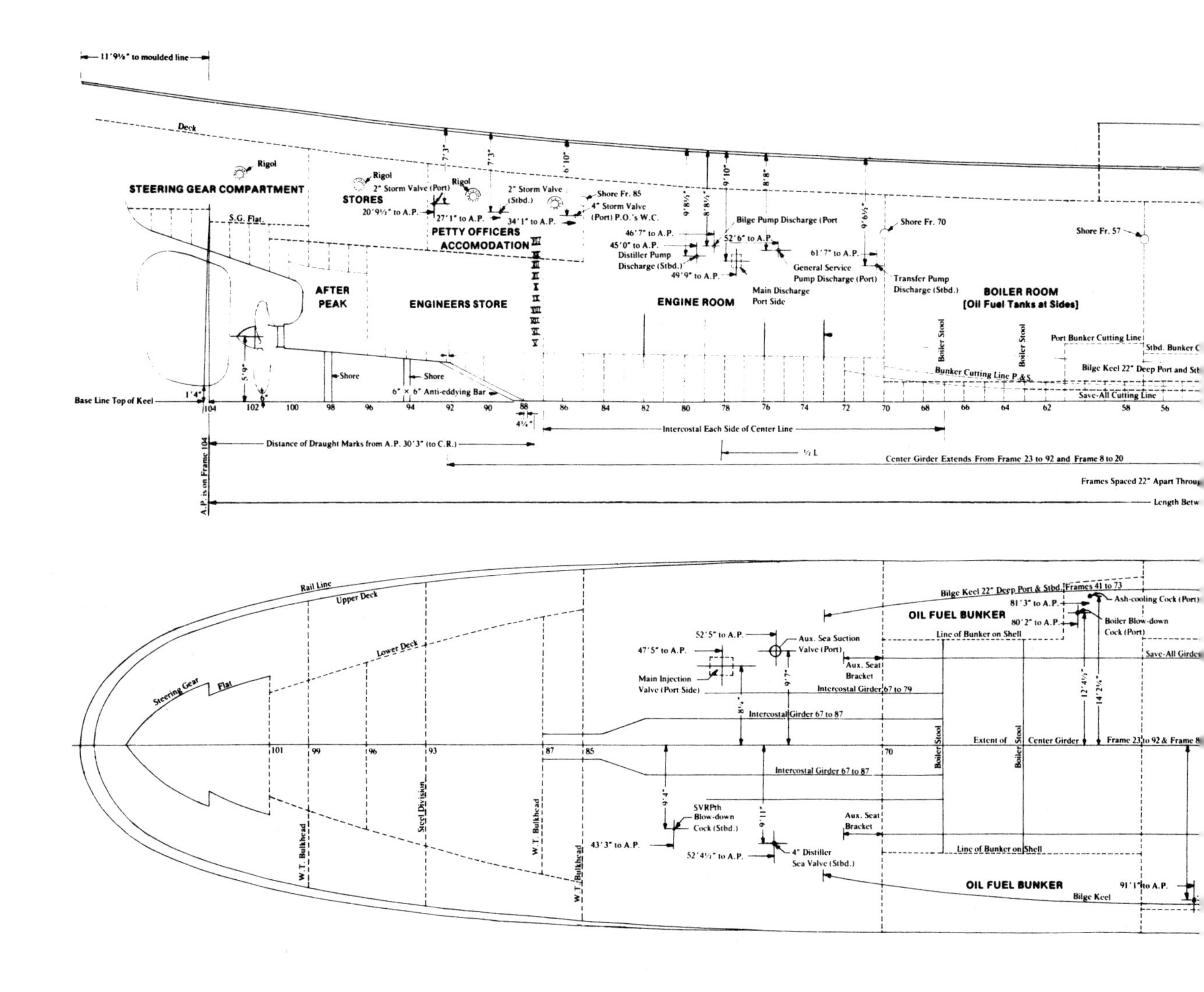

DOCKING PLAN
(as built)
H.M.S. BEGONIA
Modified by Admiralty, March 1942

DIMENSIONS
Length Overall: 205′ 1¾″
Length Between Perpendiculars: 190′ 0″
Breadth Extreme: 33′ 1⅝″
Depth Moulded: 17′ 6″

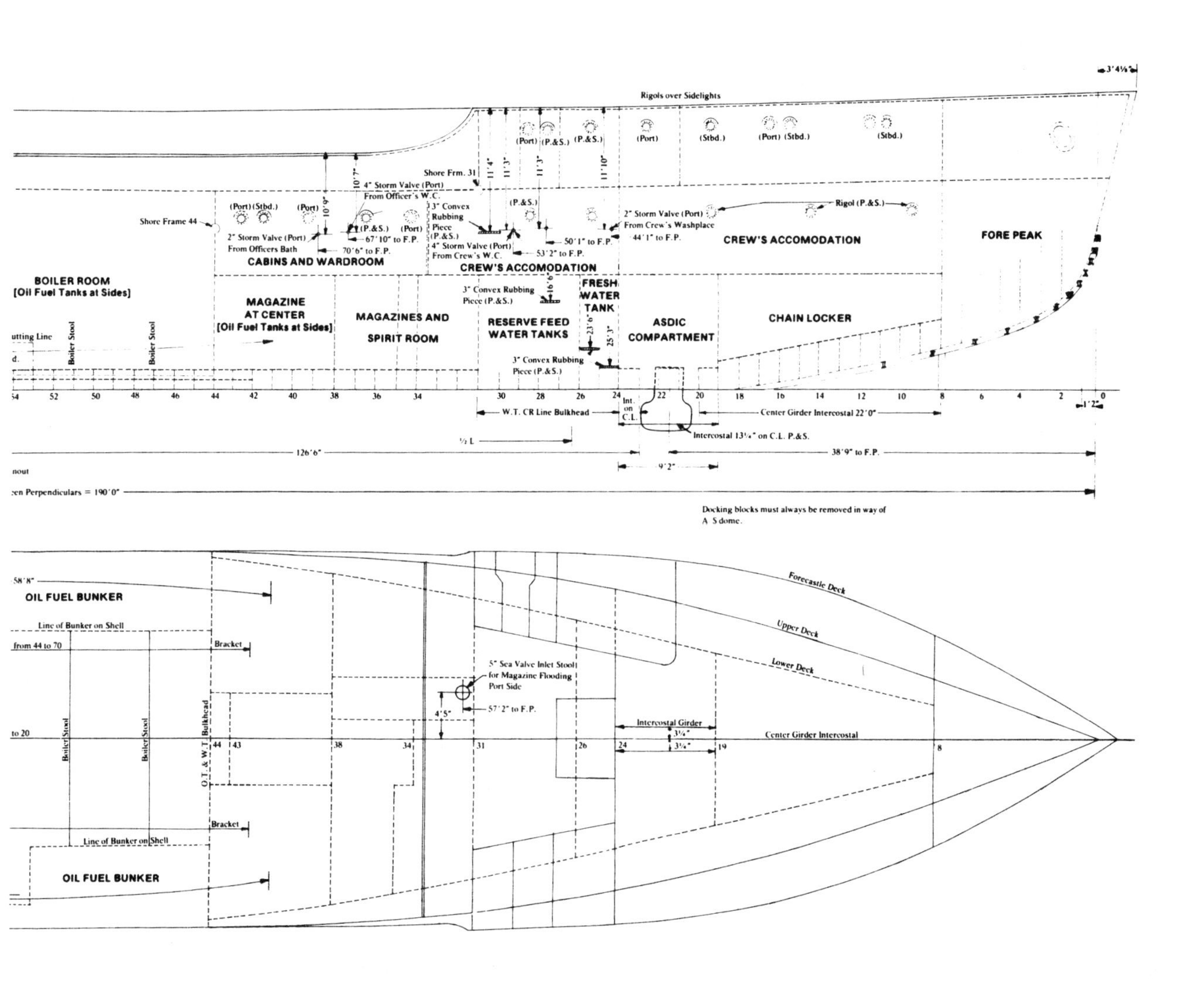

N.B. All vertical and thwartship dimensions given on this plan are girths.

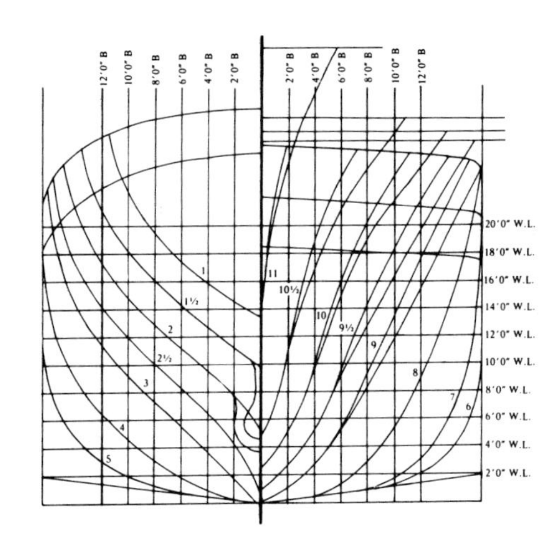
12'0" B
10'0" B
8'0" B
6'0" B
4'0" B
2'0" B
2'0" B
4'0" B
6'0" B
8'0" B
10'0" B
12'0" B
20'0" W.L.
18'0" W.L.
16'0" W.L.
14'0" W.L.
12'0" W.L.
10'0" W.L.
8'0" W.L.
6'0" W.L.
4'0" W.L.
2'0" W.L.
1
1½
2
2½
3
4
5
11
10½
10
9½
9
8
7
6

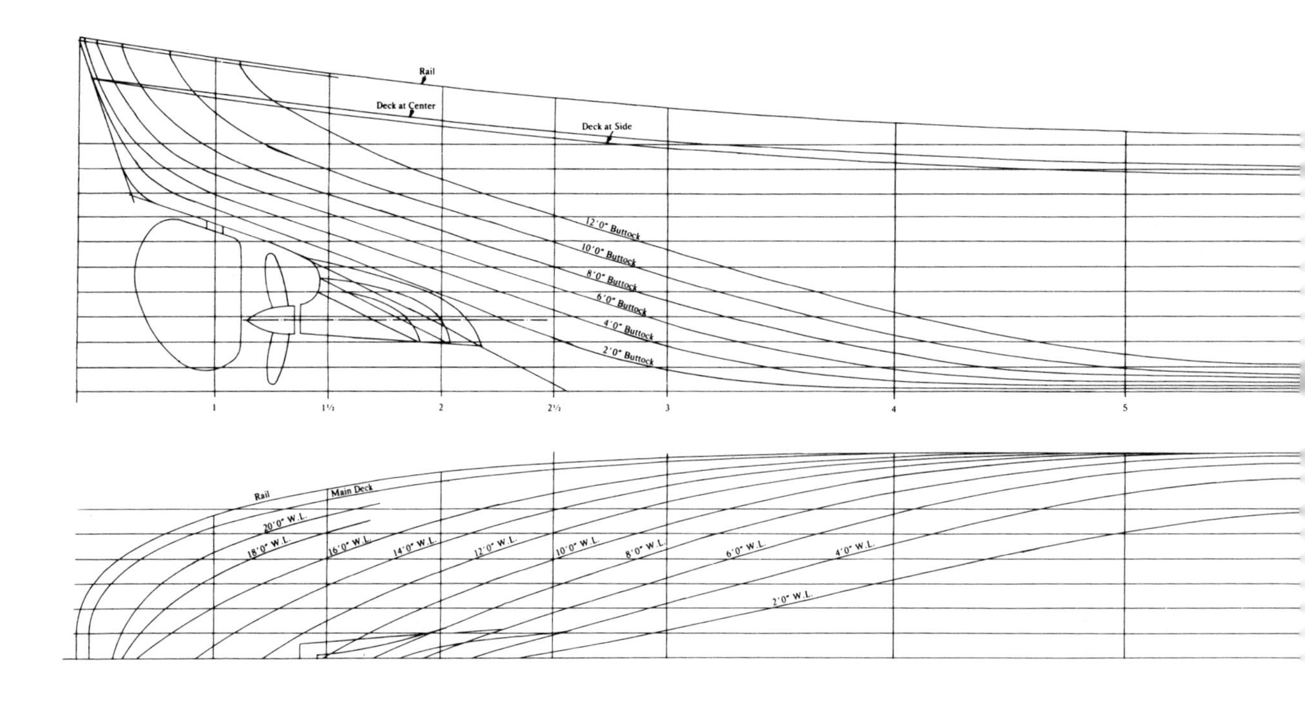
Rail
Deck at Center
Deck at Side
12'0" Buttock
10'0" Buttock
8'0" Buttock
6'0" Buttock
4'0" Buttock
2'0" Buttock
1
1½
2
2½
3
4
5
Rail
Main Deck
20'0" W.L.
18'0" W.L.
16'0" W.L.
14'0" W.L.
12'0" W.L.
10'0" W.L.
8'0" W.L.
6'0" W.L.
4'0" W.L.
2'0" W.L.

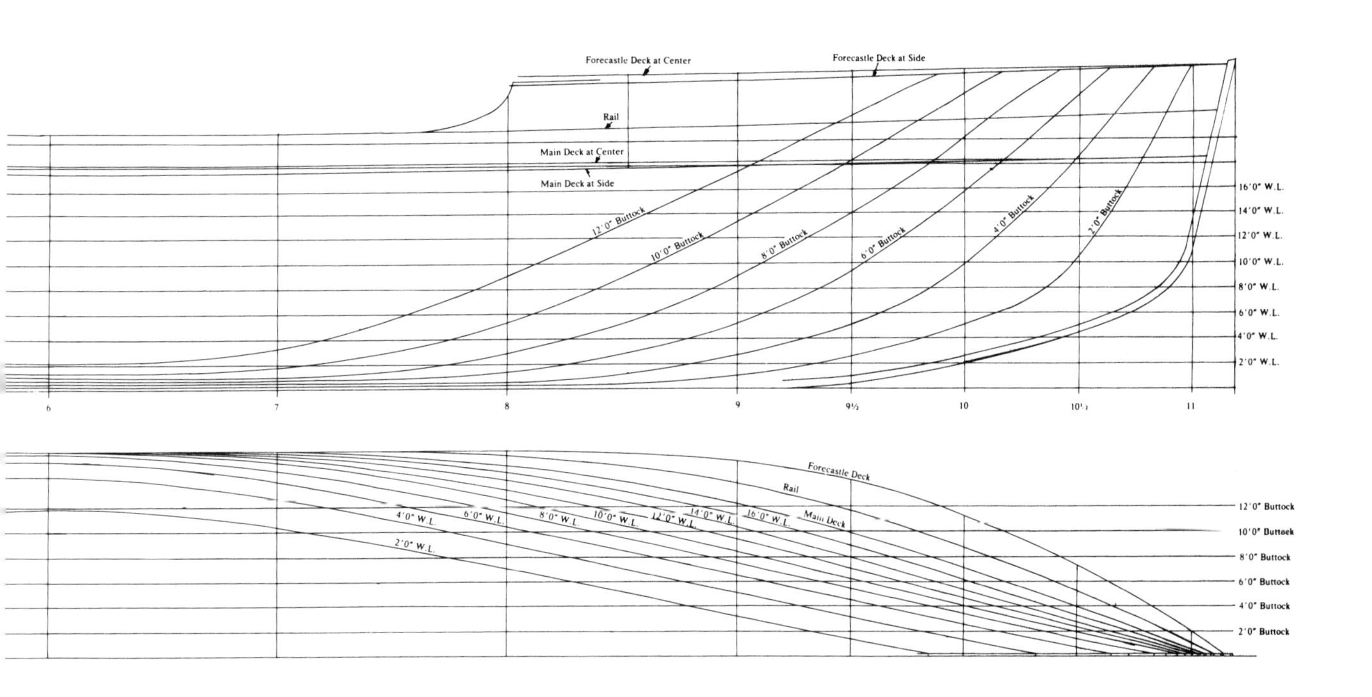
Forecastle Deck at Center
Forecastle Deck at Side
Rail
Main Deck at Center
Main Deck at Side
12'0" Buttock
10'0" Buttock
8'0" Buttock
6'0" Buttock
4'0" Buttock
2'0" Buttock
16'0" W.L.
14'0" W.L.
12'0" W.L.
10'0" W.L.
8'0" W.L.
6'0" W.L.
4'0" W.L.
2'0" W.L.
6
7
8
9
9½
10
11
Forecastle Deck
Rail
Main Deck
4'0" W.L.
6'0" W.L.
8'0" W.L.
10'0" W.L.
12'0" W.L.
14'0" W.L.
16'0" W.L.
2'0" W.L.
12'0" Buttock
10'0" Buttock
8'0" Buttock
6'0" Buttock
4'0" Buttock
2'0" Buttock

The Type 123 Asdic head and compartment of HMCS ALBERNI, 1941. These were fitted by Special Admiralty teams at first then RCN technical teams in 1942 to wars end. The raising and lowering winch can be seen to the left, with the Asdic head dead center. The wrenches and boxes were used in replacing an oscilator head, the component most prone to failure, usually from too shallow depth charge drops by the carrying ship. The anti-submarine hut was usually immediately behind the Asdic compartment. [via author]

ASDIC

An Asdic wheel-lock, as it appeared in the Asdic/chart house on an early corvette. This item was manned by an Asdic operator, who, wearing headphones, would turn the spokes of the wheel-lock to turn the oscillator head in the Asdic dome under the hull. The geared shaft can be seen going down from the geared wheel. The gauge below the wheel is an indicator, telling how many degrees to port or starboard the head is turned. The top portion is a binnacle compass which was used to give a relative bearing to the contact and could also be used by the officer on watch to check the course being steered by the helmsman, one deck below. The switch signalled an underwater contact, which in most cases resulted in action stations. The voicepipes lead to the wheelhouse below. [via author]